Let me start out by saying "Welcome!"

Welcome to the beginning of a new chapter of your life. Within these pages lies transformative knowledge that can unlock unparalleled growth, understanding of yourself & others, & can set you on a course towards inner peace. I tell you this as someone who has personally benefited in remarkable ways from this wisdom, & I encourage you to dive into this book with an open mind & an open heart.

Chris's ability to articulate concepts in such powerful & profound ways has helped guide me on my life's journey, & I am deeply honored to share with you both his impact on my life & bear witness to the beginning of his knowledge's effect on your journey as well. His words can help shed light on your path, especially in the dark times of our human experience.

Again, I speak from a place of great honor because Chris has been a bright & gentle glow of enlightenment as I have made my way out of the darkest time of my life. His analogies & his words have given me phrases & concepts to grasp & nurture as I have struggled to find my strength & voice again.

Draw strength from those that have gone before you & are shining the light back for those that want to follow. I encourage you to walk alongside others & share this amazing message of hope, especially on your social media as we continue on this exciting adventure forward.

The first time I heard Chris talk about "the Villagers," I was absolutely captivated. The analogy was simple yet potentially life-changing. He has spent years honing this concept. Not just as an idea, but as a tool to help others navigate their inner worlds as it did for him.

In this book he combines wisdom, humor, & an extraordinary gift for making the complex feel accessible. We dive deep into the human experience, breaking down emotions, thoughts, & behaviors into relatable & actionable insights. With every chapter, he guides readers toward becoming the leader of their own internal village.

Chris's work is not just a framework for understanding yourself—it's a roadmap to healing, self-mastery, & inner peace. As you turn these pages, prepare to be challenged, comforted, & inspired. More than anything, prepare to meet yourself in a way you never have before.

It is my great honor & privilege to introduce to you these precious treasures … both the book & its author … Chris Hinton

3

ISBN : 979-8-21858032-2

Who's Talking?

Chris Hinton

To everyone who believed in me,

To those I've shared my story with,
who listened not just with open ears but with open hearts.
To the ones who looked me in the eye,
smiled, and said, "You should write a book."

This is for you.

For every word of encouragement you gave me
when I doubted myself.
For every moment you reminded me that my story
was worth telling, even when I couldn't see it.
You saw something in me that I couldn't yet see in myself,
and your belief became a spark that lit the fire for this book.

This book exists because of you—
your faith, your kindness, and your
willingness to hear my truth and tell me it mattered.
Thank you for being my sounding boards,
my motivators, and my cheerleaders.
Thank you for giving me the courage
to put this out into the world.
This is as much yours as it is mine.
You gave me the gift of belief,
and I hope this book gives something
meaningful back to you.

Thank you for your support by purchasing this book
and for giving me the opportunity to walk
alongside you on your journey.
I hope the ideas and tools within these pages serve you well,
offering clarity, insight, and a deeper connection to yourself.
Your trust in this work means the world to me,
and I'm grateful to be a part of your growth.

- Chris Hinton -

"No man ever steps in the same river twice, for it's not the same river and he's not the same man"

- Heraclitus

Table of Contents

Part 1: Building Awareness and Understanding the Framework

    1. Welcome to Your Village
    2. The Observer Awakens
    3. The Morning Meeting:
       Who's Running the Show Today?

Part 2: Identifying and Managing Key Villagers

    4. The Villager of Anger
    5. The Addicted Villager
    6. I'm a Recovering Narcissist,
       and You Probably Are Too

Part 3: Navigating Emotional Dynamics and Relationships

    7. Boundaries Are Bridges
    8. The Villager of Covert Contracts
    9. The Myth of Control
    10. Relationships as Kickball
    11. Entitlement vs. Empowerment

Part 4: Advanced Emotional Awareness

    12. Illuminating Emotional Blindspots
    13. Letting Go of "Should"
    14. The Rebellious Villager
    15. Abandonment and Rejection
    16. Depression
    17. Identity

Part 5: Healing and Moving Forward

    18. Trauma and Resilience
    19. Emotional Contracts and Expectations
    20. When the Village Falls Silent
    21. The Villager of Self-Sabotage
    22. Being Open in the Moment
    23. The Power of Grief

Part 6: Mastery and Leadership

    24. Calm is Contagious
    25. The Villager of Forgiveness
    26. Healing
    27. Honorable Mentions
    28. Reclaiming Your Staff and Leading
       Your Village Forward

Who's Talking ?

Have you ever felt overwhelmed by your emotions? Maybe you've reacted to something in the heat of the moment and later wondered, Why did I do that? Or perhaps you've found yourself stuck in the same destructive patterns, even when you desperately wanted to change. The truth is, most of us don't know what's really driving our thoughts and behaviors. That's because we're not paying attention to who's talking.

Imagine, for a moment, that your inner world is a village. It's not just any village—it's **your** village, full of unique and colorful characters. Each one represents a different emotion, thought, or belief that you've ever experienced. There's the villager of anger, stomping around with a megaphone, and the villager of joy, dancing in the town square. Some villagers are helpful and kind, while others are loud, impatient, or downright destructive. And then there's you—the observer, the leader of this village. You're the one who decides how the villagers interact and who holds the staff of control.

But here's the catch: if you're not paying attention, one of your villagers might snatch the staff and take over. That's when anger lashes out in traffic, fear convinces you to stay small, or shame whispers that you're not enough. It's not that these villagers are bad—they're just doing what they think is best for you. The problem is, they're not supposed to run the show. That's your job.

The Thought Experiment
If you were to take your age and multiply it by 365 days in a year, you would come up with a number we'll call **X**. This is close to the total amount of lived days you've had on this planet. Some of these days may have been uneventful, while others were full of emotional experiences that you stored deep inside your psyche. And every day, you take a new refugee in with your new lived experiences. These experiences, whether joyful, traumatic, or otherwise significant, still influence the way you

This book isn't about digging through your past for answers you may never find. It's about helping you take back your village. It's about recognizing the villagers who are causing chaos, understanding their motives, and learning how to lead them to freedom.

At its core, this book is about teaching you how to meditate—not in the traditional sense of just sitting in silence, but in every waking moment of your life. Whether you're stuck in traffic, in the shower, working at your desk, or even in the middle of an argument, this framework will guide you toward a meditative awareness of yourself and your emotional world.

Life is a series of choices, but the options you see before you are limited by the level of consciousness you exist in at any given moment. The goal of this book is to help you raise your awareness so that you can see more possibilities, more paths, and more options than you ever realized were available. When I look back over my own life, I can see that the choices I made were always constrained by my level of awareness at the time. I wasn't blind, but I couldn't see beyond my own emotional point of view. And that's the point—there were moments when I simply couldn't do better because I didn't know better. My hope is that this book will help you wake up to new possibilities that have been surrounding you all along but were camouflaged by the limitations of your current awareness.

Your subconscious mind is one of the most powerful tools you have, yet for so long, it has been hidden from you. The reasons you do what you do may not be clear, even to yourself. For example, maybe as a child, you felt abandoned or unseen. Perhaps you were taught that love was conditional—that it had to be earned through achievement or perfection. These experiences can create subconscious blind spots that shape how you show up in relationships. Without realizing it, you may find yourself striving to be the perfect partner, terrified that if you don't measure up, the person you love will leave you. The irony is that this fear-driven behavior often sabotages relationships, leading to the very outcomes you feared. When that relationship ends, you move on to someone new, carrying the same blind spots and repeating the same patterns, reinforcing a false narrative that you are unlovable or broken.

But this isn't the truth. You aren't broken—you just have blind spots. You've told yourself stories about who you are based on experiences that don't define you. They were moments in time, not the full picture of your identity. My goal in writing this book is to help you uncover those blind spots, challenge those stories, and reconnect with the authentic version of yourself that's been waiting beneath the surface.

What you'll find here is not just a guide to understanding your emotions; it's a roadmap to expanding your awareness. It's a framework that will help you pause, observe, and lead your villagers with compassion and clarity. This isn't just about emotional regulation; it's about waking up to the infinite possibilities that exist when you learn to step out of autopilot and into conscious living. My hope is that by the time you finish this book, you'll not only know your villagers—you'll also know yourself. And in knowing yourself, you'll discover a deeper connection to the world around you and to the people you love.

As a life strategist, I've come to realize that everything in life revolves around relationships. The relationship you have with food, friends, family, money, health, fitness, and even the relationship you have with yourself—all of it is interconnected. Everything we do is relational at its core.

Improving these areas of your life begins with improving your relationship with yourself. If you can learn to navigate your inner world more effectively, you'll naturally see the ripple effect in how you relate to everything else—your habits, your loved ones, your finances, your health, and your fitness. It all starts within, and the better you get at understanding and leading yourself, the better every other relationship in your life will become.

So, let's begin. It's time to take back your village, raise your awareness, and wake up to the life that's been waiting for you.

"The journey of 1000 miles begins with a single step"

-Lao Tzu

Part 1:

Building Awareness & Understanding the Framework

"Knowing yourself is the beginning of all wisdom."

– Aristotle

Chapter 1

- Welcome to Your Village -

(Awareness)

When you think about your life, do you ever wonder what's going on behind the scenes inside your mind? Why certain emotions or thoughts dominate your day while others seem distant or silent? Imagine, for a moment, that your inner world is a bustling village, filled with characters who represent every emotion, thought, and experience you've ever had. These characters are your villagers.

Each villager has a role, a voice, and an agenda. Some villagers are loud, demanding your attention—like the villager of **anger** who shouts for justice or the villager of **fear** who whispers warnings of danger. Others, like **joy** or **curiosity**, may be quieter, waiting for the right moment to emerge. And then there are the villagers who sit silently in the background, holding the weight of your past—**grief**, **shame**, or **unspoken desires**. Together, they create the symphony of your inner life, each contributing to the cacophony or harmony depending on who is in charge.

The observer. You are not a villager but the one tasked with overseeing the entire village. Picture yourself holding a staff, standing atop a cliff, looking out over the villagers below. As the **observer**, you are the leader, the one responsible for guiding and harmonizing these voices. Yet, like any leader, your presence is crucial. Without you, the village can descend into **chaos**, with the loudest villagers taking over while others are silenced, ignored, or forgotten.

But what happens when the **observer** is absent? When you lose sight of your role as the leader of your emotional village? Let's dive into a story that might feel all too familiar.

Emma's Bad Day

Emma woke up feeling irritable. She hadn't slept well, her mind had been restless with worry, and the stress of work loomed over her like a dark cloud. As she got ready for the day, little frustrations started piling up—a coffee spill, a forgotten task, an unanswered email. By the time she was on her commute, her patience had worn thin. When another driver cut her off, Emma's heart raced, and without hesitation, her villager of **anger** *stepped up. Before she could even think,* **anger** *took the wheel—Emma slammed on her horn, yelled, and felt the adrenaline surge through her veins. The rest of the day followed this pattern. Emma was short with her coworkers, snapped at a friend over text, and even felt a pang of* **guilt** *when her dog greeted her joyfully after work, but she couldn't muster the energy to respond. She felt disconnected, as though she was on edge and didn't know why.*

In this moment, Emma's **observer** *was absent. Her villagers—***anger**, **frustration**, *and* **resentment** *—had taken* **control** *of the village, each amplifying the chaos while silencing the voices of* **reason**, **compassion**, *and* **self-awareness**. *Without the* **observer**, *Emma felt trapped in the storm of her emotions, unable to find her way back to her* **peace**.

Awakening the Observer

The key to peace, as Emma would later learn, lies in awakening the **observer**. Unlike the villagers, the **observer** doesn't react; it responds. The **observer** is not driven by impulse but by awareness. Imagine if, in the moment that the other driver cut her off, Emma had paused and asked herself, **"Who's talking?"** Instead of reacting with **anger**, she might have recognized that her villager of **frustration** was triggered by her already strained morning. By acknowledging the voice, she could have chosen to respond differently—perhaps by taking a deep breath and letting the moment peacefully pass by, without letting it define her day.

Your villagers will always be there, each vying for **control**, sometimes even shouting over one another. But with practice, you can learn to recognize their voices and decide who gets to speak, who needs to wait, and who needs to step back entirely. The journey you're about to embark on is not about silencing your villagers; it's about learning to lead them with **compassion**, **clarity**, and **wisdom**.

Throughout this process, you'll discover that your power lies in your ability to observe, understand, and guide. Your **observer** is not an emotion, but the one who can look at your emotions and choose how to respond. It's the **calm** in the storm, the leader of the village, and the one who holds the staff. Awakening your **observer** is not only possible—it's liberating!

Reflective Questions:
1. Who are some of the villagers you recognize in your own life? Are they loud and demanding, or quiet and reserved?
2. How often do you feel like your **observer** is awake versus asleep? How do you know?
3. Think of a recent moment where a villager took over. How could the **observer** have handled it differently?

This journey begins with awareness.

Welcome to your village.

"Between stimulus and response, there is a space. In that space lies our power to choose our response. In our response lies our growth and our freedom."

– Viktor Frankl

Chapter 2

- The Observer Awakens -
(Self-Discovery)

As we begin to explore your emotional village, let's focus on the **observer**—the quiet, wise leader within you. The **observer** is not defined by any single villager. It doesn't react out of **fear**, **anger**, or **sadness**. Instead, it pauses, assesses, and responds with clarity.
But what happens when the **observer** is awake? Let's follow Emma and her journey to awaken her **observer**.

Emma Learns to Pause
*A week after a particularly bad day, Emma decided it was time to try something new. The next time she felt **anger** rising within her, she paused and took a deep breath. Then she asked herself*
*the key question: **"Who's talking?"***
*The answer was immediate—it was the villager of **anger**, loud and fiery. But as Emma sat with this question, she began to notice something deeper. Behind the **anger**, she felt the villager of **hurt** quietly lurking. Emma realized that **anger** often acts as the bodyguard of **hurt**. The person who had cut her off in traffic that morning hadn't just made her angry—they had made her feel **disrespected**.*
*And that sense of **disrespect** triggered something far older, a wound from her past that still lingered in her emotional village. By recognizing this connection, Emma found she could begin to let go of the **anger** and focus on healing the **hurt** instead.*

Your Observer in Action
Awakening your **observer** is like strengthening a muscle—it takes practice, consistency, and intentional effort. Just as you wouldn't expect to be incredibly strong after a single workout, cultivating your **observer** requires repetition and mindful awareness over time. At first, it might feel

"By failing to prepare, you are preparing to fail."

– Benjamin Franklin

Chapter 3

- The Morning Meeting: Who's Running the Show Today? -

(Mindfulness and Leadership)

Every village needs a leader, and every leader needs a plan. Without one, the villagers run wild, each trying to seize the staff and take **control**. That's why starting your day with a "Morning Meeting" can make all the difference. It's a moment to pause, check in with your villagers, and set the tone for your day. Think of it as a team huddle before the game—only this time, you're the coach, the players, and the referee. Let's see how Emma learned to implement the Morning Meeting in her life.

Emma's Experiment with Mindfulness

Emma used to wake up and immediately dive into her day. She'd scroll through her phone, check emails, and mentally list all the things she needed to do. By the time she got out of bed, the villager of **overwhelm** *had already claimed the staff, and her day felt chaotic before it even started.*

One morning, Emma decided to try something different. She stayed in bed for a few extra minutes, closed her eyes, and asked herself, **"Who's talking?"** *At first, the villagers were loud and jumbled, like a room full of people talking over each other. But as she listened, she noticed the villager of* **anxiety** *was leading the charge, whispering worries about work deadlines and personal responsibilities.*

Instead of ignoring it, Emma acknowledged the villager of **anxiety** *and asked, "What do you need from me today?"* **Anxiety** *replied, "A clear plan." Emma jotted down a quick to-do list and immediately felt a sense of* **calm**. *The Morning Meeting became her new routine, a simple way to start each day with clarity and intention.*

27

The Power of the Morning Meeting

The Morning Meeting isn't about silencing your villagers; it's about giving them a chance to speak so your **observer** can decide who gets the staff. It's a moment to reflect, plan, and lead your village with purpose. By taking just a few minutes each morning to check in, you can prevent reactive villagers from hijacking your day.

Tools for a Successful Morning Meeting

1. Ask Three Questions:
    - *"Who's talking?"* Identify the loudest villagers and what they're trying to say.
    - What do they need? Acknowledge their concerns and see if you can address them.
    - What's my intention for the day? Decide how your **observer** will lead the village.
2. The "5-Minute Journal": Start your day by writing down three things you're grateful for, three things you want to accomplish, and one positive affirmation. This simple practice helps you focus on what matters most.
3. Visualize Your Village: Picture your villagers sitting around a table, each waiting their turn to speak. Let them voice their concerns, but make it clear that your observer has the final say.

Modern-Day Challenges to Mindfulness

In a world of constant distractions, staying mindful can feel like an uphill battle. The villager of **validation** wants you to check social media likes, while the villager of **responsibility** urges you to tackle your overflowing inbox. These distractions make it harder to hear your villagers clearly, let alone lead them effectively.

Creating a **boundary** around your morning such as leaving your phone on airplane mode or delaying email checks—can give your **observer** the quiet space it needs to take charge.

A Funny Twist on the Morning Meeting

Imagine your villagers literally gathering for a morning meeting. The villager of **doubt** shows up in pajamas, holding a coffee mug that says, "Don't talk to me until I've catastrophized." Meanwhile, the villager of **optimism** enthusiastically presents a color-coded chart of your goals. Letting your **observer** gently mediate between these extremes can turn a chaotic scene into a productive one.

Reflective Questions:
1. What's your current morning routine, and how does it impact your day?
2. Which villager tends to take over your mornings? How can you guide them more effectively?
3. What's one small step you can take tomorrow to start your day with clarity and intention?

Part 2:

Identifying & Managing Key Villagers

"Speak when you are angry, and you will make the best speech you will ever regret."

– Ambrose Bierce

Chapter 4

- The Villager of Anger -

(Awareness and Understanding)

Anger is one of the loudest villagers in the village. It doesn't knock on the door or politely wait its turn—it storms in, flips over tables, and yells, "Pay attention to me!" And for good reason. **Anger** isn't inherently bad; it's a signal, like a smoke alarm, alerting you to something deeper happening. But if left unchecked, it can burn your village to the ground. **Anger** often masks other emotions, acting as a bodyguard for feelings like **hurt**, **fear**, or **shame**. The key to managing **anger** is to understand that it's not the enemy. It's just a villager doing its best to protect you. Let's see how Emma learns to deal with her villager of **anger**.

Emma Faces Her Anger

Emma was having what she thought would be a peaceful evening at home. She had her favorite show queued up, a bowl of popcorn in her lap, and a cozy blanket wrapped around her.
But as she scrolled through her email, she spotted a passive-aggressive message from her boss. "Could you please follow up on the report I asked for three times last week?" it read. Emma's face flushed with heat, her jaw clenched, and before she knew it,
*the villager of **anger** was at the helm.*
*The villager of **anger** wanted to fire back immediately with a scathing reply. But Emma paused, took a deep breath, and asked herself,*
***"Who's talking?"** She realized it wasn't just **anger**—it was **hurt**. The email made her feel **unappreciated** and **disrespected**,*
*and **anger** had stepped in to protect her from those feelings.*
*Instead of sending a heated response, Emma decided to step into her **observer** role. She drafted a **calm**, professional reply and saved it as a draft to review later. By the time she revisited it,*

*the villager of **anger** had quieted down, and Emma felt proud of how she handled the situation.*

The Role of Anger in Your Village
Anger is often misunderstood. It's not just about rage or yelling; it's about **boundaries** and protection. When someone crosses a **boundary**, **anger** rushes in to defend you. The problem arises when **anger** becomes the default response, overshadowing other emotions like **sadness** or **fear**.

Remember, **anger** is your smoke alarm; it just tells you something needs attention. It's up to your **observer** to investigate, address the root cause, and to solve the problem.

Tools for Managing the Villager of Anger
1. The "Cool Down" Rule: Before responding in **anger**, give yourself a cooling-off period. This could be five minutes, an hour, or even a day. Use this time to ask yourself, ***"Who's talking?"***
2. Identify the Bodyguard: When you feel **angry**, dig deeper. Is there another emotion hiding behind it? **Hurt**? **Fear**? **Disrespect**? Naming the underlying emotion can help you address it directly.
3. Channel Your Energy: **Anger** generates a lot of energy. Instead of letting it spiral, channel it into something productive, like a workout, cleaning, or writing out your thoughts.

Modern-Day Triggers
In today's fast-paced world, **anger** gets triggered by everything from a slow internet connection to someone cutting in line at the grocery store. The villager of **anger** loves these moments, but they're rarely worth losing your **peace** over.

For example, imagine you're in a drive-thru line, craving your favorite coffee, and the person in front of you is taking forever. The villager of **anger** screams, "Hurry up!" But your **observer** steps in and says, "It's just coffee." Take a breath. By choosing to stay **calm**, you prevent a minor inconvenience from ruining your day.

A Funny Twist on Anger

Let's lighten things up. Have you ever tried to assemble furniture from a certain Swedish store? If you have, you've probably met the villager of **anger**. There you are, staring at incomprehensible instructions and wondering why you have three extra screws. The villager of **anger** mutters, "Burn it all, Burn it to the ground!" But your **observer** gently reminds you, "This isn't life or death. Just take a break and come back later."

By learning to laugh at these moments, you give yourself the space to respond with patience instead of frustration.

Reflective Questions:
1. Think of a time when **anger** took **control**. What was the deeper emotion behind it?
2. How does **anger** show up in your life? Is it a bodyguard for another villager?
3. What tools can you use to manage **anger** the next time it storms through your village?

"We cannot solve our problems with the same thinking we used when we created them."

– Albert Einstein

Chapter 5

- The Addicted Villager -
(Compassion for Struggles)

Imagine walking through your village and seeing a villager stumbling around, clearly struggling. This is the villager of **addiction**. It's tempting to point fingers, to **isolate** or **shame** them. But **addiction** is not the defining feature of a person—it's a part of their village, not the whole. We all have our struggles, and for some, **addiction** becomes a loud, persistent voice in the village.

Addiction isn't just about substances like alcohol or drugs. It can take the form of gambling, seeking validation, overindulgence in food, obsessing over social media, or even clinging to toxic relationships. The truth is, we all wrestle with some form of **addiction**, whether we realize it or not.

Addiction Is a Struggle with Self-Soothing

Addiction isn't merely about having an "addictive personality." More often, it's rooted in difficulty with self-soothing. When faced with **discomfort** or **pain**, many of us reach for something external to make it go away—food, drugs, attention, or even our smartphones. But these external fixes often exacerbate the problem, creating a cycle of dependence that's hard to break.

Take Emma, for example. After a stressful day juggling work and her responsibilities, she turned to her usual "comfort"—a bottle of wine and hours of reality TV. It wasn't that she loved the wine or the TV shows; it was that she didn't know how to deal with the tension and emptiness inside her. Her villager of **avoidance**, *disguised as her* **addiction**, *was in* **control**.

Compassion for the Addicted Villager

The first step in addressing **addiction** is recognizing that the **addicted** villager is not your enemy. They are a part of you that's trying, in their own flawed way, to help you cope. When we treat **addiction** with **shame**—believing it makes us **"bad"** or **"weak"**—we only feed its power. Instead, approach your **addicted** villager with **compassion** and **curiosity**. Ask, "What are you trying to soothe? What are you **afraid** of ?"

By understanding the underlying needs and emotions fueling **addiction**, you can begin to address them directly, rather than numbing them. **Addiction** is often not the problem itself, but a response to **unmet needs**, **unresolved pain**, or deep **emotional discomfort**. It may be an attempt to soothe feelings of **loneliness**, cope with unresolved **trauma**, or escape from overwhelming **stress** or **anxiety**. For example, someone may turn to substances, behaviors, or habits as a way to fill a void left by unacknowledged **grief**, **fear**, or a **lack of connection**. When you take the time to uncover these hidden driving forces, you can start to meet those needs in healthier ways—whether it's seeking support, practicing **self-compassion**, or developing new coping mechanisms. This process doesn't just address the symptoms of **addiction** but also helps you reconnect with your inner self, allowing you to heal the root causes rather than masking the **pain**.

Reclaiming Control

As you strengthen your **observer**, you'll start to recognize when the **addicted** villager is trying to take over. This awareness allows you to pause and ask, "***Who's talking?***" Instead of reacting impulsively, you can choose a healthier way to respond—whether it's going for a walk, journaling, or simply sitting with the discomfort and allowing it to pass.

It's important to remember that **addiction** doesn't define you. You are not your **addiction**, just as you are not your **anger**, **fear**, or **sadness**. These are parts of your village, and you, as the **observer**, have the power to lead them with **compassion** and **clarity**.

Reflective Questions:
1. What are some things you turn to when you're feeling **stressed** or **overwhelmed**?
2. How can you approach your **addictive tendencies** with **compassion** rather than **shame**?
3. What is one small, healthier choice you can make the next time your **addicted villager** tries to take control?
4. Who in your life struggles with their own problems in ways that invite you to share in their **addiction** or help them burn down their village?
5. The next time you reach for something you feel is unhealthy or counterproductive, pause, take note, and honor that you've caught a glimpse of the pattern. What do you think is causing you to lean on this **addiction** to cope with adversity?

This book is my attempt to help you learn yourself because you are a unique individual and no one else is like you. Whether the **addiction** is food that started at a young age or **isolation, self doubt, internal shame**, drugs, gambling, or relationships, we must stay vigilant, protect ourselves, and learn how to maneuver through our difficult times.

"The greatest deception men suffer is from their own opinions."

– Leonardo da Vinci

Chapter 6

- I'm a Recovering Narcissist, and You Probably Are Too -
(Self-Awareness)

We live in a world where the word **"narcissist"** is thrown around often, usually as an insult. But what if we redefined it? What if **narcissism** wasn't about being a bad person, but instead, about a particular villager in our emotional village—one that seeks **validation**, **control**, and a **sense of self-worth**? The truth is, we all have **narcissistic tendencies**. We all have moments where we focus too much on ourselves, driven by our own unmet needs and unhealed wounds.

This chapter isn't about labeling or condemning. It's about **self-awareness** and **healing**. By recognizing our own **narcissistic** villagers, we can start to lead them with **compassion** and prevent them from taking over the village.

The Broken Mirror
Imagine looking into a mirror that's been shattered into hundreds of pieces. Each piece reflects a part of you—your emotions, behaviors, and experiences. Now, imagine picking up one piece and saying, "This is all of me." That's what happens when we let one villager define our **identity**.

For some, the **narcissistic** villager becomes that piece of glass. It's the part of us that **seeks approval**, **thrives on recognition**, and **struggles with insecurity**. But here's the truth: you are not just one piece of broken glass. You are the whole mirror. Recognizing this helps us move beyond **shame** and **judgment** and into **understanding** and **growth**.

Emma's Narcissistic Villager

*Emma always prided herself on being a supportive friend, but recently, a close friend told her, "You have a way of making things about you, even when they're not." The comment stung, and at first, Emma was defensive. "That's not true!" she thought. But later, as she reflected, Emma realized there was some truth to the statement. Her **narcissistic** villager had a habit of shifting conversations to her own experiences, not because she didn't care, but because she craved **validation**. Once Emma recognized this, she began asking herself during conversations,* **"Who's talking?"** *By doing so, she could quiet her **narcissistic** villager and focus on genuinely listening to others.*

Observing Narcissistic Tendencies

Recognizing our own **narcissistic tendencies** doesn't mean we're bad people. It means we're human. **Narcissism** often arises from **unhealed trauma** or **unmet expectations**. The villager that seeks **validation** is trying to protect us from feelings of **inadequacy** or **rejection**. The key is **awareness**. When you notice this villager taking over, pause and ask, "What do you need?" By understanding its motives, you can lead it with **compassion** rather than letting it run unchecked.

A Superpower in Relationships

As you become better at observing your own villagers, you'll also become more skilled at recognizing who's running the villages of others. This **awareness** allows you to navigate relationships more effectively by understanding the emotional dynamics at play. For example, imagine sending your villager of **vulnerability**—a part of you that seeks **connection**, **honesty**, and **trust**—into a conversation with someone whose village is dominated by their **narcissistic** villager. The **narcissistic** villager thrives on **control**, **self preservation**, and **deflecting blame**, making it unlikely to create the safe environment your **vulnerable** villager needs.

In this situation, your **vulnerability** might be met with **dismissal**, **manipulation**, or even **criticism**, leaving you feeling **hurt** or **rejected**. Recognizing this mismatch ahead of time allows you to adjust your approach. Instead of leading with **vulnerability**, you might engage with **curiosity**, **patience**, or even healthy **boundaries**, protecting your own villagers from unnecessary harm.

This skill is invaluable in relationships—whether personal or professional—because it helps you assess emotional safety and compatibility. It's not about judging others or suppressing your own villagers but about learning when and how to share parts of yourself in ways that foster connection and minimize conflict. Over time, this understanding enables you to decide whose villages are worth engaging with and which ones might require a little distance for your own emotional well-being. This **awareness** becomes a superpower. This protects you from unnecessary **hurt** while fostering deeper connections.

I Challenge You

Take a moment to step outside of yourself and look at your actions from an outside perspective. Review times and circumstances where you acted in a selfish, self-absorbed, self-protective, or insecure ways to get what you wanted. It could be something small—a comment you made to get attention, a time you interrupted someone because you felt your story was more important, or a moment where you prioritized your needs over others without considering the impact on them.

The goal of this challenge isn't to **shame** you. It's to help you see that we all have parts of us that we struggle with. Sometimes those parts emerge in ways that look very ugly to others, even if we don't recognize it at the time. By becoming aware of these moments, you can begin to understand your own villagers, including the **narcissistic** villager, and lead them with **compassion** instead of letting them take over.

Reflective Questions:

1. What moments in your life reveal your own **narcissistic tendencies**?
2. How can you approach your **narcissistic** villager with **curiosity** and **compassion**?
3. Think of someone you've labeled as a **narcissist**. What might their villagers be struggling with?
4. When you acted selfishly or self-absorbed in the past, what **unmet needs** or **insecurities** were driving that behavior?
5. What steps can you take to pause and observe your behavior the next time you feel this villager trying to take over?

Part 3:

Navigating Emotional Dynamics & Relationships

"Daring to set boundaries is about having the courage to love ourselves, even when we risk disappointing others."

– Brené Brown

Chapter 7

- Boundaries Are Bridges -

(Protecting Relationships and Yourself with Love)

Boundaries often get a bad reputation. People think of them as rigid walls or ultimatums meant to keep others out. But healthy **boundaries** aren't barriers—they're bridges. They allow others to connect with you in a way that is **safe**, **respectful**, and **nurturing**. **Boundaries** show people how to navigate your emotional village without stepping on landmines, and they protect your relationships and well-being from unnecessary harm.

Setting **boundaries** is an act of **love**—for yourself and for others. It's a way of saying, "I care about this relationship enough to show you where my limits are so we can avoid damaging it." Also, **boundaries** protect your personal energy, emotions, and time, ensuring that your villagers don't become **overwhelmed** by **chaos** or **conflict**.

Let's explore how Emma learned to set **boundaries** that strengthened her connections and protected her peace.

Emma's Lesson in Boundary-Setting

*Emma valued her friendships deeply, but she had one friend, Sarah, who often pushed her emotional limits. Sarah would call late at night, venting about her problems without asking if Emma was available or in the right headspace to listen. Emma's villager of **guilt** would always step in, urging her to answer the phone and be a good friend, even if it left her feeling drained and resentful.*
One night, after a particularly long call, Emma realized she couldn't keep sacrificing her own well-being to meet Sarah's needs. She asked herself, **"Who's talking?"** *The villager of **resentment** whispered, "She doesn't care about your time."*

But Emma knew that wasn't true—Sarah simply didn't know she was crossing a line.
The next day, Emma decided to set a **boundary**. She told Sarah, "I love being here for you, but late-night calls are hard for me. Let's plan a time to talk during the day when I can be fully present." To Emma's surprise, Sarah was understanding and appreciated her honesty. Their friendship grew stronger because Emma communicated her limits with care.

An Experiment for Connection

When it comes to relationships, whether romantic, familial, or platonic, setting **boundaries** and improving communication can feel challenging. Here's an experiment that I believe could be a game-changer for couples counseling or resolving complications with friends and family:

For one moment, imagine that you and the other person are not the problem. Instead, you are two leaders—the observers of your respective villages. You are both CEOs of companies meeting over lunch to discuss the challenges your employees (villagers) are facing. The goal isn't to blame the other CEO or criticize their leadership. Instead, the conversation focuses on the behaviors of the villagers: "When your employees speak to my employees in a certain way, my employees feel a certain way about that."

This analogy reframes the dynamic, disarming defensiveness and encouraging collaboration. By proposing this approach, it removes personal blame and instead fosters curiosity: "Why do your villagers behave this way?" " What's causing my villagers to react this way?" This shift allows both parties to work together as equal leaders, brainstorming solutions to help their villagers (emotions and reactions) communicate and interact more effectively. The focus moves away from you are the problem to let's explore how our villagers are impacting this dynamic.

I truly believe this approach has the potential to revolutionize the way couples approach conflict in therapy. It creates a safe, lighthearted space to discuss challenges while preserving the dignity and value of both partners. By working together to get their "employees" to collaborate better, couples can improve connection, communication, and trust in their relationships.

Boundaries Protect, Not Punish

Healthy **boundaries** aren't about **controlling** others—they're about protecting your village. Imagine a **boundary** as a line with landmines behind it. When someone crosses that line, they risk stepping on a landmine—your emotional triggers. For example, if your boundary is "Do not yell at me," and someone raises their voice, it might trigger your villager of **anger** or **hurt**, leading to an explosive reaction.

The purpose of a **boundary** is to prevent these explosions, not to punish the other person. By clearly communicating your **boundaries**, you're giving others a roadmap to your village. This helps avoid unnecessary conflict and allows for deeper, healthier connections.

Boundaries aren't just about protecting yourself—they're about protecting the relationship as well. If you care about someone, you show them where the landmines are so they can avoid accidentally hurting you. And if they care about you, they'll respect those **boundaries** because they want to keep the relationship intact.

Are You Up for the Challenge?

Here's something to think about: When someone in a relationship triggers us with their behavior, how often do we ask them to change instead of looking inward to understand why we're triggered? It seems easier to push the burden of growth onto the other person, asking them to adjust who they are or how they behave so we can feel okay. But is that truly fair—or sustainable?

If you want to build a healthy relationship, compatibility is a great place to start. But compatibility doesn't mean you like the same music or root for the same football team. True compatibility means that when I discover something about myself that triggers me, I let you know what it is. At the same time, I don't expect you to do all the work or make all the changes. Being compatible means we both commit to the work—we meet each other halfway.

For example, imagine saying: "I don't like it when you scream during arguments or use that tone with me. It makes me scared and reminds me of the past. I don't want to hold that against you, though. I know that's how you've learned to communicate your frustration. I want to work on myself so I can be less reactive to this, and I hope you'll also try to meet me halfway. This will take effort on both our parts, but I believe we can grow through it together."

This is what true compatibility looks like. Often, people want their partners to change without doing the internal work to strengthen themselves. But if one person in the relationship has an endless list of triggers and expects the other person to change their behavior every time, that partner might eventually feel like they've lost themselves entirely.

True growth comes when both people are willing to look inward, work on their own triggers, and meet each other halfway. It's not about making the other person entirely responsible for your emotional regulation—it's about teamwork and mutual effort.

Tools for Setting Boundaries

1. The "When-Then" Formula:

    Use this structure to express your **boundaries** clearly and collaboratively: "**When** you [specific behavior], I feel [specific emotion]. I would prefer if you [specific request]. **Then** I'm going to [specific action to address my provoked areas] so we can meet each other halfway."

    Example: "When you raise your voice during an argument, I feel overwhelmed, and I would prefer if you could speak more calmly so we can better resolve things. Then I'm going to go inside myself and work on the triggered spots I notice I struggle with—like my sensitivity to tone— so I can meet you halfway and support us both in improving how we communicate."

This approach acknowledges and expresses your dislike of the specific behavior while inviting the other person to work on it with you. At the same time, the "then" portion demonstrates accountability for your own emotional triggers, showing your partner that you're willing to put in effort on your side of the relationship. This creates a balance where neither person feels like they are solely responsible for doing all the work, fostering collaboration and mutual respect.

2. Boundaries with Love:
    Frame your **boundaries** as acts of care to strengthen relationships rather than to create conflict. For example: "I want us to have a strong relationship, so I need to share this with you..."

    This approach shifts **boundaries** from being perceived as rigid or confrontational to becoming a way of fostering **trust, respect, and emotional safety**. When you express a **boundary** with **love**, you invite the other person into a partnership of mutual growth. Potential outcomes include deeper trust, healthier communication, and a stronger emotional connection. While the risk of not framing **boundaries** this way can lead to defensiveness or misunderstandings.

3. Consistency is Key:
    Boundaries lose their power if you don't enforce them. Following through with your stated limits is crucial, even if it feels uncomfortable at first. For example, if you set a **boundary** about not responding to work emails after 7 PM but still reply occasionally, it sends mixed signals, and the boundary becomes meaningless.
    Consistency reinforces clarity, respect, and trust—not just in your relationships with others but also within yourself. If you fail to

enforce your **boundaries**, the potential consequences can include **resentment**, **burnout**, and **confusion**. Conversely, consistent enforcement fosters **respect**, helps you maintain your emotional well-being, and encourages others to honor the limits you've set.

Modern-Day Boundary Challenges

In today's world, maintaining **boundaries** can feel especially challenging. Work emails at midnight, social media messages at all hours, and the pressure to be constantly available blur the lines between personal and professional life. The villager of **guilt** might nudge you to say "yes" to every request, while the villager of **obligation** might whisper, "You have to respond right away." This internal pressure can leave you feeling stretched too thin and disconnected from your true priorities.

Creating **boundaries** in the digital age might mean turning off notifications during family time, setting specific work hours, or letting friends know you'll respond when you have the mental space to do so. These small acts of self-care help protect your emotional village from **burnout**, **resentment**, and **overwhelm**. By doing this, you prioritize your well-being and ensure that you show up for others in a way that feels sustainable and authentic, rather than drained and resentful.

A Funny Twist on Boundaries

Imagine your villagers debating how to enforce **boundaries**. The villager of **patience** suggests, "Let's politely let them know our limits." Meanwhile, the villager of **anger** shouts, "BUILD A MOAT!" Your **observer** steps in with a smile, reminding everyone that **boundaries** are about connection, not isolation.

Reflective Questions:
1. What's a **boundary** you've been hesitant to set, and how might it protect your emotional village?
2. How can you frame a **boundary** as an act of **love** in your relationships?
3. How can you challenge yourself to work on your own triggers, rather than asking others to change entirely for you?

"Assumptions are the termites of relationships."

– Henry Winkler

Chapter 8

- The Villager of Covert Contracts -
(Uncommunicated Expectations)

Imagine walking through your village and coming across a quiet villager, sitting alone, waiting for someone to notice them. This villager doesn't voice their needs but silently assumes that others should already know. This is the villager of **covert contracts**—those unspoken expectations we place on others without ever communicating them.

Covert contracts are like invisible agreements where one person is fully committed, yet the other party has no idea an agreement even exists. A playful way to explain this dynamic is through the definition of stalking: "When two people go for a long romantic walk together, but only one of them knows about it."

Here's how **covert contracts** show up in daily life:
- Dating Edition: "I always listen to their problems and compliment them. Surely, they'll realize I'm the one for them." Translation: You're expecting a relationship in return for your emotional support, but they think you're just a kind friend.
- Workplace Edition: "I stayed late every night this week to help the team. My boss will definitely give me a raise." Reality: Your boss didn't promise a raise—your assumption created the expectation.
- Marriage Edition: "I cleaned the house and cooked dinner. My spouse should know this means I want some alone time later." Expecting someone to read your mind often leads to disappointment.

A clever way to think about **covert contracts** is this:
"Assuming someone knows your **covert contract** is like handing them an invisible map and blaming them for getting lost."

We're All Guilty of This

More than likely, you currently have uncommunicated expectations of a partner, friend, or family member. Maybe you expect your partner to notice when you're upset without telling them, or you believe a friend should always reach out first if they care. These unspoken expectations often lead to **disappointment**, **resentment**, and fractured relationships because they assume others can read our minds or think the way we do.

What Are Covert Contracts?

Covert contracts are unspoken agreements we create in our minds about how others should behave. These assumptions replace communication, holding others accountable for expectations they never agreed to.

For example:
- "If I take care of you without you asking, you will take care of me without me asking."
- "If I remember your birthday, you should remember mine."
- "If I'm feeling sad, you should know without me having to tell you."

The core issue with **covert contracts** is the assumption that others are telepathic. This mindset creates a default expectation that people should just know what we need.

From a young age, we learned to expect others to anticipate our needs. When we cried, someone likely comforted us. When we were hungry, someone fed us. But as adults, we have a voice—something we didn't have as infants—and it's our responsibility to use it.

Love and Relationships Are Not the Same

Before we go further, let's clarify an important distinction: **love** and relationships are not synonymous.

- You can **love** someone deeply and not be in a relationship with them.
- You can be in a relationship with someone and not **love** them.

Love is selfless and unconditional—it's wanting what's best for another person. Relationships, however, are negotiated engagements that require communication about shared values and expectations.

For instance, you may **love** a friend but choose not to pursue a close relationship due to incompatible values. Conversely, you might stay in a relationship with a coworker or family member for practical reasons, even if **love** isn't central to the dynamic.

When we conflate **love** with relationships, we often fall into the trap of covert contracts, assuming **love** should automatically meet all relational needs. Thriving relationships, however, require clear communication and **boundaries**.

The Problem with Covert Contracts

One of the biggest challenges with **covert contracts** is the unnecessary suffering they create. When expectations aren't met, feelings of **hurt**, **disappointment**, and **anger** often emerge—emotions unfairly directed at the other person, who may have no idea they've done anything wrong.

Imagine this scenario:
You spend weeks planning a surprise party for your partner. You assume they'll return the gesture for your birthday without you having to say anything. But when your birthday comes and goes without acknowledgment, you're **furious**.

This is the villager of **covert contracts** at work. Instead of expressing your desire for a celebration, you relied on an unspoken expectation that your partner couldn't possibly fulfill without being told.

Communicated Preferences

The solution isn't to eliminate expectations altogether—that's unrealistic. Instead, focus on shifting from uncommunicated expectations to communicated preferences.

When you express your preferences clearly, you give others the opportunity to meet your needs.

For example:
- Instead of assuming your partner knows you're upset, say, "I'm feeling down and could use some support."
- Instead of waiting for a friend to reach out, say, "I miss talking to you and would love to catch up soon."

This approach keeps the focus on what you can **control**—your communication. However, even when you express your needs, there's no guarantee they'll be met. Relationships involve negotiation, and the other person may not always meet your preferences.

By framing expectations as preferences rather than demands, you detach yourself from the outcome, reducing unnecessary suffering.

I Challenge You

Take a moment to reflect on your life. Can you identify a time when an uncommunicated expectation left you feeling disappointed, resentful, or even angry toward someone?

Now, ask yourself:
- Did I clearly express my need?
- Was it fair to expect the other person to know what I needed without me telling them?
- How could I have communicated my preference in a way that allowed for a healthier interaction?

Finally, challenge yourself to notice **covert contracts** as they arise in the future. Instead of assuming others should know what you need, pause and communicate your preference. Recognize that while your preferences matter, they may not always be met—and that's okay.

Reflective Questions:
1. What **covert contracts** have you created in your relationships?
2. How do these unspoken expectations affect your feelings toward others?
3. When have you felt **hurt** or **resentful** because someone didn't do something you thought they should have?

"Surrender to what is. Let go of what was. Have faith in what will be."

– Eckhart Tolle

Chapter 9

- The Myth of Control -
(Radical Acceptance)

Control is an illusion that many of us cling to in an effort to feel safe. We think, If I just plan everything perfectly, nothing will go wrong, or If I can just manage other people's behavior, my life will be easier. But the truth is, most of what happens in life is beyond our **control**. The harder we try to **control** things, the more **frustrated** and **anxious** we become. Radical acceptance is about letting go of this illusion and embracing reality as it is—not as we wish it to be. It doesn't mean giving up or not caring; it means recognizing the limits of your power and focusing on what you can influence.

This truth is difficult to accept because every villager in your emotional village operates under a shared, unspoken motto: "***I only feel OK when things go according to the way I need them to go.***" This belief is the root of **anxiety**, **frustration**, and much of the village's suffering. Let's explore how Emma learned this lesson in her own village.

Emma's Battle with Control

*Emma was a perfectionist. She prided herself on having a perfectly clean house, an organized calendar, and a tightly managed to-do list. But one weekend, her well-ordered world came crashing down. Her dishwasher broke, her dog got sick, and a surprise visit from her parents threw her schedule into **chaos**.*

*As the villager of **overwhelm** took the staff, Emma felt herself spiraling. "Why can't things just go the way I planned?" she thought. Her villager of **frustration** chimed in, pointing fingers at everyone and everything around her.*

*Emma sat down, took a deep breath, and asked herself, **"Who's talking?"** **Overwhelm** and **frustration** were shouting the loudest, but beneath them, the villager of **fear** whispered,*

"What if I can't handle this?"
*In that moment, Emma realized she was trying to **control** things she couldn't change. She decided to let go. Instead of **stressing** about the broken dishwasher, she called a repair service. Instead of worrying about the surprise visit, she embraced the chance to spend time with her parents. By focusing on what she could **control**— her mindset and actions—Emma turned a **chaotic** weekend into a manageable one.*

The Limits of Control
Trying to control everything is like stapling water, it's futile.
Life is unpredictable, and no amount of planning can prevent surprises, setbacks, or disappointments. The **observer's** role is to help you distinguish between what is within your **control** and what isn't.

The truth is, the village suffers because of the motto shared by every villager, **"I need things to be the way I need them to be in order to feel OK."** When life doesn't align with this expectation, **anxiety** arises from **helplessness** and the unknown, and **frustration** from trying to force **control** where none exists. Reframe this to, **"I need things to be, the way they be!"**

Let me illustrate this with a thought experiment: imagine life as a card game. You're seated at a table in a casino, surrounded by your friends and family. Across from you sits the dealer. You can call the dealer whatever you like: the universe, God, or fate. What matters is this: the dealer deals you the cards, and you don't get a say in which cards you receive.

Sometimes, the dealer hands you a **grief** card. Other times, it's a **betrayal** card or a **celebration** card. You can't trade these cards back, nor can you swap them with another player. The only choice you have is how you play the hand that you've been dealt.

The trouble begins when the villagers try to **control** what the dealer does. They demand different cards, or better ones, believing they **deserve** them. But make no mistake: you don't get to dictate what's dealt to you. The dealer has one job—handing out the cards—and your job is equally clear: to focus on how you play them.

This is why radical acceptance is key. **Peace** doesn't come from **controlling** the dealer; it comes from mastering the hand you've been given.

<u>Tools for Practicing Radical Acceptance</u>
1. The Control Inventory:
    - Make two lists: one for things you can **control** (e.g., your actions, your responses) and one for things you can't (e.g., other people's choices, the weather). Focus only on the first list.

2. The Serenity Question:
    - When faced with a challenge, ask yourself: "Is this something I can influence?" If yes, take action. If no, practice letting go.

3. Box Breathing:
    - When you feel **overwhelmed** by what you can't **control**, use this military technique to center yourself: breathe in for 4 seconds, hold for 4 seconds, breathe out for 4 seconds, and hold again for 4 seconds. Repeat until **calm**.

A Funny Twist on Control

Imagine your villagers trying to **control** things outside their reach. The villager of **perfection** demands the clouds part for a perfect picnic, while the villager of **worry** insists on Googling "how to make people like you" for hours. Meanwhile, your **observer** chuckles, knowing that some things—like the weather or other people's opinions—are simply out of your hands.

Reflective Questions:
1. Think of a time when you tried to **control** something outside of your influence. How did it affect your emotional village?
2. This week, what's one area of your life where you can practice letting go?
3. How can you remind yourself to focus on what's within your **control** when challenges arise?

Remember: your **peace** lies in how you play your cards, not in trying to **control** the dealer. Focus on your moves, let go of what's beyond you, and trust the process. Life is not about perfect **control** but about embracing the imperfect game.

"The meeting of two personalities is like the contact of two chemical substances; if there is any reaction, both are transformed."

– Carl Jung

CHAPTER 10

- Relationships as Kickball -
(Reciprocity and Balance)

Relationships are like a game of kickball. Both players take turns kicking, running, and catching the ball, with the shared goal of keeping the game going. But what happens if one player refuses to kick? Or if one keeps hogging the ball, leaving the other stuck waiting in **frustration**? Balance and reciprocity are at the heart of every successful relationship—whether it's with friends, family, or partners. If the game becomes one-sided, it stops being fun for everyone involved.

Let's explore how Emma discovered the importance of balance in her relationships and learned how to keep the game fair.

Emma's Lopsided Game
Emma had been dating James for a few months, and at first, everything felt perfect. James was charming, attentive, and seemed to care deeply about her. But over time, Emma noticed a pattern. She was the one making most of the effort—planning dates, checking in, and offering support whenever James needed it.
While James seemed grateful, he rarely reciprocated. One evening, after spending hours preparing a surprise dinner for James, Emma sat at the table alone, waiting for him to arrive. When he texted last minute to cancel without an apology, the villager of **resentment** grabbed the staff and shouted,
"Why do I always have to be the one to try? "
Emma paused and asked herself, **"Who's talking?"** She realized it wasn't just **resentment**—it was the villager of **exhaustion**, worn out from carrying the relationship alone. Emma **loved** James, but she knew this wasn't sustainable. Relationships, like kickball, need two active players. She decided it was time to have an honest

conversation with James about how she was feeling. To her surprise, James hadn't even realized how unbalanced things had become. He apologized and made an effort to step up, planning their next date and taking on more responsibility in the relationship. With both players back in the game, Emma felt the weight lift off her shoulders, and their connection grew stronger.

The Balance of Giving and Receiving

In healthy relationships, there's a natural rhythm of giving and receiving. This doesn't mean everything is always 50/50—sometimes one person might need more support, and that's okay. But over time, the effort should feel balanced. If one person is always giving while the other is always taking, the game becomes **exhausting** and **unsustainable**.

Reciprocity isn't just about fairness—it's about showing that you value the relationship enough to contribute to it. When both players actively participate, the relationship becomes a source of **joy** and **connection** rather than **stress** and **resentment**.

The number one reason people seek out relationships is to exchange value. You want something from the other person, and they want something from you—whether that's quality time, companionship, sexual intimacy, friendship, laughter, or shared experiences like travel. Relationships thrive when both people feel they're being "paid" in the currency that matters to them.

What complicates this is that the preferred "currency" often evolves over time. For example, one partner might value acts of service early in the relationship but later prioritize emotional support or physical intimacy. This is why conversations about balance and reciprocity are essential. Consider this: I often hear people say, "I gave this and this and did that, but it was never good enough." When I hear this, I wonder if they were trying to pay their partner in a currency that partner didn't value. Imagine going to a coffee shop, ordering a coffee, and trying to pay the cashier with another coffee instead of money. The cashier would look at you funny because they don't need more coffee—they need payment in money. The same principle applies in relationships: if you're giving something your partner doesn't value, it's unlikely to resonate.

Knowing your partner's preferred currency—the way they want to be "paid" in the relationship— is crucial. For example, you might love receiving words of affirmation, but if your partner values physical affection, you need to understand that difference. Expressing how you like to be "paid" and understanding your partner's preferences fosters mutual respect and clarity.

Here's the challenge: if you don't know how you like to be paid—or worse, if you think your partner should already know—this is problematic. It falls into the trap of assuming that **love** or effort should be intuitive. This belief is often tied to the idea of deserving something. But the truth is, we don't get what we deserve in relationships—we get what we negotiate.

Healthy relationships require clear communication about value exchange. First, learn yourself— understand your triggers, your needs, and your preferred "currency." Then, communicate those to your partner in a way they can comprehend. In turn, ask them how they would like to be paid in the relationship. By doing this, you both become active players in the game of kickball, keeping the ball moving and the connection alive.

Food for Thought Perspective:
The Business of Relationships

When you enter an intimate relationship, it's almost like starting a business. Together, you've launched a venture that we'll call the Intimate Partnership Business LLC. This foundational business represents the connection and partnership between you and your significant other. It requires care, collaboration, and effort to thrive. As time goes on, you may decide to take on additional ventures.

Perhaps you focus on careers, creating a Career Business LLC. Suddenly, you're juggling two businesses, each demanding energy and attention. Eventually, you may have children, and with that comes the Children Business LLC. Now, you're managing three businesses, each with its own demands and complexities.

Here's the challenge: most businesses rely on a structure of regional managers, general managers, store managers, and employees to ensure everything runs smoothly. But in your life, it's often just the two of you trying to manage everything. Without clear roles, communication, and intentional effort, it's easy for the Intimate Partnership Business LLC to become neglected. Over time, the relationship that started it all begins to falter. The career and children businesses take precedence, and the intimate partnership—the foundation of everything—gets put on the back burner. Without the time, attention, and effort it needs, the partnership runs the risk of going bankrupt, leaving the relationship insolvent.

This perspective reminds us of an important truth: relationships are conditional. They require intentional work, care, and value transactions on both sides to sustain themselves. Neglecting the core relationship in favor of other priorities can erode the foundation of everything you've built together. The key is to remember that while career and children businesses are important, they cannot thrive without the success of the original venture. The Intimate Partnership Business LLC must remain a priority. By nurturing your relationship with the same intentionality and teamwork as you would a business, you can ensure that it continues to thrive alongside your other ventures.

Tools for Maintaining Balance in Relationships

1. The Effort Audit:

    Reflect on your relationships and ask: "Am I giving too much? Am I giving too little?" Identify areas where the balance feels off and decide how to address them.

2. Communicate Needs Clearly:
   If you feel like the game is lopsided, have an open conversation about it. Use "I" statements to express your feelings without placing blame. For example: "I feel like I've been doing most of the planning lately. Can we work together to balance it out?"

3. Celebrate Contributions:
   Acknowledge and appreciate the effort the other person puts into the relationship. Gratitude encourages reciprocity and strengthens the connection.

Modern-Day Challenges to Balance

In today's fast-paced world, it's easy for relationships to fall out of balance. The villager of **distraction** might pull one person toward work, hobbies, or social media, leaving the other person feeling neglected. Meanwhile, the villager of **obligation** might push one partner to overcompensate, taking on more than their fair share to keep the relationship afloat. By staying mindful and communicating openly, you can navigate these challenges and keep the game of kickball enjoyable for both players.

A Funny Twist on Relationships as Kickball

Imagine your villagers playing kickball together. The villager of **over-giving** keeps running back and forth, kicking and catching the ball alone, while the villager of **apathy** sits in the outfield picking flowers. Your **observer** steps in, handing both players a whistle and reminding them that it takes teamwork to win the game.

Reflective Questions:
1. Think of a relationship in your life that feels unbalanced. What changes could you make to restore reciprocity?
2. How can you communicate your needs without blaming the other person?
3. What "currency" do you prefer to be paid in, and how can you express this to your partner?

Chapter 11

- Entitlement vs. Empowerment -
(Choosing Your Path)

In every village, there are voices that shape the way we navigate life. Two of the loudest and most disruptive are *the Villager of* **Entitlement** *and the Villager of* **Victimhood**. These villagers often team up, creating a powerful duo that keeps you stuck, frustrated, and far from where you want to be. Understanding their influence—and learning how to replace them with the empowering villager of **resilience**—is key to creating the life you want.

The Villager of Entitlement: "I Deserve"
The Villager of **Entitlement** thrives on the belief that the world owes you something. It shouts phrases like, "I deserve better," or, "This isn't fair," and when unmet expectations arise, it **rages**, **blames**, and retreats into **resentment**. The Villager of **Entitlement** convinces you that happiness, respect, or success should arrive gift wrapped on your doorstep simply because you exist. It demands **recognition** without effort, respect without reciprocation, and an easy life without action.

But here's the truth: **entitlement** is a trap. It places your happiness and success in the hands of others or the universe. It says, "I'll only be okay if people or circumstances meet my demands," which leaves you feeling **powerless** when those demands aren't met. Instead of moving forward, you stew in **frustration**, wondering why life isn't delivering what you believe you're owed.

Entitlement often grows from unmet needs or distorted expectations. Perhaps, as a child, you were told, "You're special and deserve the best," without being taught the effort required to achieve it. Or maybe you've experienced hardship, and **entitlement** became your way of reclaiming

control. Regardless of its origin, the Villager of **Entitlement** thrives on the false belief that the world owes you something.

The truth? The world owes you nothing. Not **love**. Not respect. Not success. Everything worth having is something you create, negotiate, or nurture.

The Villager of Victimhood: "It's Not My Fault"
The Villager of **Victimhood** is just as cunning but operates differently. Instead of demanding, it wallows, mournfully sighing, "Why does this always happen to me?" or, "It's not my fault." It casts **blame** outward, avoiding responsibility and fostering a sense of **helplessness**. While **Entitlement** demands it's happiness from others, **Victimhood** absolves you of all accountability, making excuses for your inaction and stagnation.

A **victim mentality** is a cunning disguise for **self-sabotage**. It keeps you in a perpetual loop of personal torment, convincing you that external forces **control** your life. You may find yourself stuck, blaming others or your circumstances while refusing to take the steps necessary to move forward. Think of it like driving with the parking brake engaged. The car struggles to move, and instead of releasing the brake, you curse the road for being too rough. The parking brake represents the **victim mentality**—an internal barrier—while blaming the road mirrors the act of externalizing responsibility.

Here's the hard truth: **Victimhood** feels safe because it absolves you of responsibility, but it also steals your agency. It convinces you that you're powerless when, in reality, you hold the key to your own progress.

Empowerment: The Quiet Villager Who Leads
Empowerment is the quiet, steadfast villager who reminds you that while you can't **control** everything, you always have **control** over how you show up. **Empowerment** doesn't demand or **blame**—it acts. It

recognizes that setbacks, challenges, and disappointments are inevitable, but instead of dwelling on what's owed or unfair, it asks, "What can I do with what I have? How can I respond in a way that aligns with my values?"

While **Entitlement** and **Victimhood** keep you stuck, **Empowerment** propels you forward. **Empowerment** doesn't ignore challenges or pretend life is fair. It acknowledges reality and focuses on what you can **control**—your actions, mindset, and resilience. It's not about suppressing your needs or desires but about recognizing that fulfillment starts with you, not what others give to you.

Empowerment encourages **gratitude** over **resentment**, **perseverance** over **complaint**, and **self-accountability** over external **blame**. It's the villager that builds bridges, fosters resilience, and turns obstacles into opportunities. While **Entitlement** and **Victimhood** keep you trapped in the past, **Empowerment** helps you embrace the present and take ownership of your future.

The Dance Between Entitlement, Victimhood, and Empowerment

It's easy to see how these villagers can take turns running the show. Imagine a failed job interview. The Villager of **Entitlement** might say, "I deserved that job—they should have hired me!" while the Villager of **Victimhood** might chime in with, "It's not my fault they didn't see my potential. The system is rigged." Both villagers keep you stuck in **resentment** and **frustration**, blaming external factors instead of taking actionable steps to improve.

Now imagine **Empowerment** steps in. It says, "I didn't get the job, but what can I learn from this experience? How can I improve for the next opportunity?" **Empowerment** shifts the focus from **blame** into action, helping you grow and move forward.

Shifting from "I Deserve" to "I Create"

Let's explore some common **entitlement** and **victimhood** statements and how they can be reframed into **empowerment**:

1. "I deserve recognition."
    Reframe: *"I create value that earns recognition."*
2. "People should respect me."
    Reframe: *"I create **respect** by setting **boundaries** and modeling **respect**."*
3. "Life should be easier."
    Reframe: *"I create **resilience** to handle life's challenges."*
4. "Why does this always happen to me?"
    Reframe: *"I create change by learning from my experiences and taking action."*
5. "I deserve **love**."
    Reframe: *"I create **love** through consistent effort, kindness, and care."*

The Challenge: Releasing the Parking Brake

Take a moment to locate something in your life where you feel stuck. Ask yourself:
- "What am I **blaming** on others or my circumstances?"
- "What small step can I take to create change for myself?"

Write down one **entitlement** or **victimhood**-driven belief and reframe it into an empowering action.

For example:
- **Victimhood**: "I'll never get out of this situation—it's not my fault."
- **Empowerment**: "I create new opportunities by taking small steps forward every day."

Conclusion: **Empowerment** Sets You Free

Entitlement and **Victimhood** bind you to external forces, leaving you at the mercy of others or your circumstances. **Empowerment** frees you to take ownership of your life, guiding your village with clarity and strength.

The choice is yours: Will you let the Villagers of **Entitlement** and **Victimhood** control your village, or will you lead them with **Empowerment**? Remember, the power to create the life you want is always within your hands. Start today by choosing **empowerment** over **entitlement** and **victimhood**—your village will thank you!

Reflective Questions:
1. When was the last time you felt **entitled** to something or **blamed** others for a situation? What would the Villager of **Empowerment** have encouraged you to do instead?
2. What current challenge in your life are you attributing to external factors? How can you shift your focus to what is within your **control** to create change?
3. Reflect on a time when you overcame a setback by taking ownership of the situation. How did it feel to act with **empowerment** rather than **entitlement** or **victimhood**?
4. What small, consistent actions can you take today to align yourself with the Villager of **Empowerment**, moving closer to the life you want to create?

"The world owes you nothing. It was here first."

– Mark Twain

Part 4:

Advanced Emotional Awareness

"What we see depends mainly on what we look for."

– John Lubbock

CHAPTER 12

- Illuminating Emotional Blindspots -
(What You Don't See Can Hurt You)

Emotional blindspots are the hidden corners of your psyche where unseen villagers quietly influence your thoughts, feelings, and actions. These blindspots operate like invisible threads, weaving patterns of **misunderstanding**, **frustration**, or even **pain** into your daily life. They are not flaws or failures—they are simply areas that have yet to be illuminated by your **observer**.

Uncovering emotional blindspots is essential for personal growth, emotional intelligence, and healthier relationships. The **observer's** role is to bring these hidden villagers into the light, allowing you to see how they influence your village and giving you the power to address them with **curiosity** and **compassion**.

Emma's Awakening to Blindspots

Emma had always prided herself on being generous, giving her time and energy freely to the people she cared about. But lately, she noticed a recurring pattern: when others didn't reciprocate her effort, she felt **hurt** *and* **unappreciated***. After planning a surprise party for a friend who barely acknowledged it, the villager of* **resentment** *stormed into her thoughts.*
"Why do I even bother? No one ever does this for me."
Instead of reacting, Emma paused and asked herself, ***"Who's talking?"***
Resentment *was loud, but beneath it, she uncovered the villager of* **expectation***. She realized she had been giving with the unspoken hope of receiving something in return—a* **covert contract** *she hadn't even recognized. This blindspot had been quietly shaping her actions for years, leading to repeated* **frustration** *and* **disappointment***.*

*By bringing this blindspot into the light, Emma could adjust her approach to giving, ensuring it came from a place of **authenticity** rather than hidden **expectations**.*

*On another occasion, Emma noticed a similar emotional reaction after a friend canceled dinner plans. The villager of **insecurity** whispered, "They don't care about you. You're not important." But as Emma sat with this feeling, she discovered the villager of past **rejection**, carrying childhood memories of being left out. Her reaction wasn't about her friend—it was about an unresolved blindspot tied to those early experiences. By awakening her **observer**, Emma could separate her past from her present and respond to the situation with **understanding** rather than **withdrawal**.*

Understanding Emotional Blindspots

Blindspots often stem from unexamined beliefs, unmet needs, or past experiences. These hidden villagers quietly shape how you view yourself, others, and the world, influencing your reactions in ways you may not immediately notice. Some common examples include:

- **Fear of Rejection**: Avoiding conflict because a hidden villager associates disagreement with being excluded.
- **Overworking**: Believing your worth is tied to productivity, driven by a villager that equates success with **love** or validation.
- **Distrust**: Struggling to trust others due to a villager holding onto past betrayals.

Blindspots act like invisible barriers, keeping you stuck in old patterns. But once they are illuminated, they lose their power. Recognizing a blindspot is like shining a flashlight into a dark room—it may not fix everything instantly, but it reveals what you're working with.

Tools for Uncovering Blindspots
1. *Ask "Why" Five Times*
   When you notice a strong emotional reaction, ask yourself why. Then ask why again, and again, until you reach the root cause.

   For example:
- "Why am I upset my friend canceled dinner?"
   "Because it feels like they don't care about me."
- "Why does that bother me?"
   "Because it makes me feel unimportant."
- "Why do I feel unimportant?"
   "Because I felt left out as a child."

This process helps the hidden villager step into the light.

2. *Feedback from Trusted Allies*
   Sometimes, others can see your blindspots more clearly than you can. Ask someone you trust, "What's something you think I might not see about myself?"

3. *Journaling for Insight*
   Write about a recent situation where you felt **stuck**, **frustrated**, or **confused**. Reflect on what beliefs, fears, or expectations might have influenced your reaction.

4. *Mindful Reflection*
   Imagine gathering your villagers and asking, "Who's running the show right now?" Let them step forward one by one, and listen to their voices.

Modern-Day Blindspots

In today's world, blindspots often manifest in unique ways. Social media, for example, fuels **comparison** and **validation** blindspots. You might scroll through your feed and think, "I'm not doing enough," without realizing this thought stems from a villager tied to **insecurity** or **fear** of being left behind.

Work environments can also expose blindspots. A colleague's criticism might sting more than it should because it hits a wound tied to **self-worth**. Recognizing these triggers allows you to respond thoughtfully rather than react emotionally.

A Funny Twist on Blindspots

Imagine your villagers trying to hide their blindspots:
The villager of **denial** wears sunglasses at night, muttering, "Nothing to see here." The villager of **fear** hides behind a curtain, whispering, "Let's not talk about this." Meanwhile, your **observer** steps in with a flashlight, saying, "Come on out—I just want to talk."

Humor softens the discomfort of self-discovery, making it easier to face what's hidden.

Awakening the Observer

Blindspots can only be illuminated when your **observer** is active. The **observer** doesn't judge or react; it's **curious** and **compassionate**, eager to understand the why behind the what. Awakening the **observer** also means embracing the idea that you don't know what you don't know. This humility creates space for growth and transformation.

By bringing light to your blindspots, you take the first step toward breaking old patterns, healing unresolved wounds, and creating a village that aligns with your values and goals.

Reflective Questions:
1. What's a recurring pattern in your life that might point to an emotional blindspot?
2. Who in your life could help you uncover blindspots you might not see?
3. How can you practice **curiosity** and **compassion** as you explore your hidden villagers?

"Don't demand that things happen as you wish, but wish that they happen as they do happen, and you will go on well."

– Epictetus

CHAPTER 13

- Letting Go of "Should" -
(The Danger of Unrealistic Expectations)

The word should is one of the most powerful and problematic words in your village. It's often the voice of a villager who insists that life, people, and circumstances conform to an idealized version of reality. I **should** have done better. They **should** have been kinder. Life **should** be fair. While **should** can sometimes inspire self-improvement, more often than not, it creates **frustration**, **disappointment**, and **resentment** when reality doesn't match your expectations. Letting go of **should** isn't about lowering your standards—it's about aligning your expectations with reality. It's about accepting life as it is, not as you wish it to be, while still striving for growth and change where it's possible.

Emma and the "Should" Spiral

Emma had been looking forward to her birthday dinner for weeks. She'd made a reservation at her favorite restaurant, invited a small group of friends, and imagined a perfect evening of laughter, great food, and celebration. But when the night arrived, things didn't go as planned.
One friend canceled at the last minute,
the restaurant was out of her favorite dish,
and the server spilled a drink on her new dress.
As Emma drove home, the villager of **resentment** *took the staff and started whispering, "It* **should** *have been perfect. My friends* **should** *have cared more. The server* **should** *have been more careful."*
The more she replayed the evening in her head,
the more upset she became. But then Emma paused and asked herself,
"Who's talking?" *She realized it wasn't just* **resentment** *—it was the villager of* **expectation**, *clinging to an idealized version of her birthday that reality could never match. Emma took a deep breath and decided to let go of* **should**. *Instead of focusing on what went wrong,*

she chose to remember the effort her friends made to celebrate her, and the laughs she did share with them.

The Problem with "Should"

The word should creates a covert contract with reality, one where you expect the world to behave according to your rules. When reality doesn't comply, the villagers of **anger**, **disappointment**, or **sadness** often take over. The problem isn't wanting things to go a certain way—it's the insistence that they must.

Some of the wisest philosophers and spiritual leaders from the past have expressed to us that the root cause of all suffering is expectations. I would like to take a step further and propose that the root cause of all suffering is preference. I'm not saying you shouldn't have preferences, but I want you to understand this: if you have an attachment to an outcome from a preference and it does not go your way, you will suffer. Hoping that it doesn't rain or that you get the corner office or that someone speaks to you in the way you think they **should**—these are all preferences. It would be nice if these things worked out for you, but if they don't, that ought to also be okay. Having an attachment to an outcome is a surefire way to invite more suffering into your life. These are the moments when the **observer** becomes most powerful. The **observer** doesn't cling to the past or attach to the future. The **observer** exists here and now, mindful and present, enjoying life as it unfolds without trying to **control** it. Instead of trying to **control**, reframe your perspective to simply experiencing what is.

By letting go of **should**, you free yourself from the trap of unmet expectations and open yourself to the possibilities of what is. This doesn't mean you stop striving for better; it means you stop suffering when things don't go your way.

Tools for Letting Go of "Should"

1. Reframe the Narrative:

    When you catch yourself saying **should**, reframe it with could or might. For example: "They **should** have helped me" becomes "They could have helped me, but they didn't, and that's okay."

2. Practice Radical Acceptance:

    Ask yourself: What can I **control** in this situation, and what do I need to let go of? Focus your energy on what you can change and release the rest.

3. The Gratitude Shift:

    Instead of focusing on what **should** have happened, list three things you're grateful for in the situation. Gratitude shifts your perspective from lack to abundance.

Modern-Day "Should" Triggers

In today's hyperconnected world, the villager of **comparison** thrives on **should**. Social media fuels the narrative that your life **should** look a certain way. "You **should** have the perfect relationship, the perfect career, the perfect body." But what you're seeing is a curated highlight reel—not reality.

Recognizing these triggers and stepping into your **observer** role helps you break free from the cycle. The **observer** reminds you that your journey is unique, and there's no universal script for how life should unfold.

A Funny Twist on "Should"

Imagine your villagers holding a town hall to debate all the," **shoulds**" in your life. The villager of **perfection** demands that every day **should** be productive, while the villager of **rest** argues for naps and lazy Sundays. The villager of **chaos** throws in a wild suggestion: "**Should** we just set everything on fire and start over?" Your **observer** steps in with a smile, gently reminding everyone that life doesn't have to follow a script.

Reflective Questions:
1. What's a "**should**" you've been holding onto recently, and how has it affected your emotional village?
2. How can you reframe that should into something more empowering or realistic?
3. What's one small step you can take to practice letting go of unrealistic expectations this week?

"Introduce a little anarchy. Upset the established order, and everything becomes chaos. I'm an agent of chaos."

– The Joker

CHAPTER 14

- The Rebellious Villager -
(Resisting Control)

Imagine walking through your village and spotting a villager standing apart from the rest, arms crossed, glaring at anyone who dares to approach. This is the **rebellious** villager—the one who doesn't like being told what to do, bristles at authority, and often feels the need to push back just because they can. This villager can be a fierce protector of your autonomy and authenticity, but they can also lead you astray, creating unnecessary conflict or sabotaging your progress.

The **rebellious** villager is not inherently bad. Like every other villager, they exist for a reason. But when this villager takes **control** of the village, they can cause **chaos**, leaving you to deal with the consequences. Understanding and leading this villager with **compassion** is key to keeping them in check.

The Origins of the Rebellious Villager

The **rebellious** villager often develops as a response to experiences where autonomy was threatened or taken away.

- Childhood Experiences: Perhaps you grew up with overly strict parents or teachers who dismissed your independence. The **rebellious** villager may have been born as a way to protect your sense of self.

- Innate Need for Autonomy: Humans crave independence. When we feel **controlled**, this villager rises up to assert our freedom, even when the **control** is meant to help.

- Fear of Vulnerability: Following someone else's lead requires trust and vulnerability. The **rebellious** villager often resists these feelings, fearing they will result in harm or loss of **control**.

The Double-Edged Sword of Rebellion
The **rebellious** villager has both strengths and weaknesses.

Positive Aspects:
- Standing Up for Yourself:
    This villager ensures you don't let others take advantage of you or stifle your individuality.
- Challenging Unfair Systems:
    The **rebellious** villager questions authority and challenges the status quo, often driving personal and societal growth.
- Authenticity:
    They prioritize staying true to who you are, rejecting blind conformity.

Negative Aspects:
- Self-Sabotage:
    They may resist even healthy guidance or rules, causing you to undermine your own success.
- Unnecessary Conflict:
    Constant **rebellion** can lead to friction in relationships and professional settings.
- Rebellion for Its Own Sake:
    Sometimes this villager fights back simply because they dislike being told what to do, even when the direction is helpful.

Understanding the Rebellious Villager

The **rebellious** villager isn't trying to ruin your life—they're trying to protect your independence and autonomy. The key is understanding their motivations and triggers.

- **What Does the Villager Want?**

  The **rebellious** villager desires respect and freedom. Ask yourself: What is this villager trying to protect?

- **What Triggers Them?**

  The **rebellious** villager reacts strongly to situations that feel **controlling** or restrictive. Identifying these triggers can help you manage their responses.

Strategies to Lead the Rebellious Villager

Rather than suppressing the **rebellious** villager, you can lead them with **compassion** and strategy.

- Negotiate with Them:

Instead of fighting against the **rebellious** villager, engage them in dialogue.

  Ask: "What do you need to feel respected in this situation?"

- Reframe Authority:

Help the villager see that not all rules or guidance are about **control**. Some rules exist to support growth or safety.

  - Example: "This workout plan isn't about restricting you; it's about **empowering** you to feel stronger and healthier, which is actually the goal you set out to accomplish."

- Balance Autonomy with Collaboration:

Encourage the villager to compromise. Instead of rejecting a rule outright, find a way to adapt it to align with your values.

The Danger of Unchecked Rebellion

While **rebellion** can be **empowering**, constant resistance comes at a cost:

- Isolation:

Over time, pushing back against everyone and everything can alienate loved ones or colleagues.
- Missed Opportunities:

Rejecting advice or structure can cause you to miss chances for growth or success.
- Burnout:

Fighting every perceived restriction is exhausting and often counterproductive.

Encouraging Healthy Rebellion

The **rebellious** villager can be a valuable ally when guided effectively.
- Pick Your Battles:

Teach the villager that not every situation requires **rebellion**. Save their energy for moments that truly matter.
- Channel **Rebellion** Productively:

Focus their energy on meaningful causes or goals. Advocate for yourself respectfully rather than lashing out at authority.
- Cultivate Trust:

Sometimes **rebellion** stems from mistrust. Help the villager recognize when trust is warranted, allowing them to let go of unnecessary resistance.

Reflective Questions:
1. When has your **rebellious** villager protected you in a positive way?
2. When has your **rebellious** villager caused unnecessary conflict or **self-sabotage**?
3. What triggers your **rebellious** villager to resist **control** or authority?
4. How can you balance your need for autonomy with collaboration and **trust**?

5.   What small step can you take to lead your **rebellious** villager with **compassion** rather than letting them run wild?

I Challenge You

If you recognize the **rebellious** villager in yourself, I challenge you to observe their actions the next time they rise up. Instead of reacting impulsively, pause and let your observer take control by **rebelling** against the **rebellion**!

Ask yourself: What is the **rebellious** villager trying to protect?

Evaluate: Is this **rebellion** serving my best interests, or is it **self-sabotage**?

"You are never alone. You are eternally connected with everyone."

– Amit Ray

Chapter 15

- Abandonment and Rejection -

(The Wounded Villagers)

In the quietest corner of the village, hidden beneath a porch, sits the wounded villager of **abandonment**. This villager doesn't shout or demand attention. Instead, it runs and hides, afraid to engage with the world. It fears forming new relationships and dreads losing the ones it already has. **Abandonment** is the villager that feels safest in isolation, convinced that it's only a matter of time before it will be left again.

Rejection is often the precursor to feelings of **abandonment**. While **abandonment** feels like being left behind, **rejection** feels like being pushed away—excluded or dismissed by someone or something you care about. These two villagers often work together, reinforcing one another's **pain** and **fears**.

Think back to a time when you felt **abandoned** or **rejected** as a child. Perhaps a parent left, emotionally or physically, or you were excluded from a game or scolded harshly by a caregiver. In those moments, your inner child internalized a belief: "I am not enough. I am unworthy of **love** or connection." Those early experiences became villagers, settling deep within your psyche.

As an adult, when something happens—a breakup, an argument, or a loss—these villagers are triggered. The villager of **rejection** hands the staff to **abandonment**, whispering, "See? This always happens to us." The wounded villagers retreat to their hiding places, and you're left feeling as though you're reliving those childhood wounds all over again.

Modern-Day Rejection

In our daily lives, **rejection** often feels deeply personal, but many times, it isn't. We tend to project the meaning of rejection onto our **identity**, allowing it to shape how we see ourselves.

Instead of recognizing **rejection** as situational, we internalize it as evidence of our inadequacy.

For example:
- Being **rejected** for a date: You may feel as though you were **rejected** as a person, but in reality, the other person wasn't **rejecting** you—they were declining the idea of a relationship or date with you, perhaps due to their own preferences, timing, or circumstances. It's not a reflection of your worth as a whole.
- Being **rejected** for a job interview: You might think this means you're not good enough, but in truth, you were simply not selected for that particular role. This doesn't mean you're a failure or unworthy of success.
- Being excluded from a social group: This can bring up memories of childhood exclusion, but it's often more about the dynamics of the group than a direct rejection of you as a person.

Rejection might show up when:
- A job application is denied, triggering feelings of **inadequacy**.
- A romantic partner withdraws, reigniting the **fear** of being unlovable.
- A social group excludes you, reminding you of childhood moments of being left out.

In these moments, the villager of **rejection** hands the staff to **abandonment**, whispering, "See? This always happens to us."
The key to addressing modern-day **rejection** is to recognize that **rejection** often says more about the other person, situation, or context than it does about your value or worth. It's not personal, even though it feels that way.

The Truth About Abandonment and Rejection
Here's the simple truth: as an adult, you cannot be abandoned in the same way you were as a child. You have agency now. You have power. What you're experiencing in the present moment is an echo of the past—a cry from your inner child, who is still afraid of being left behind or rejected. This isn't a weakness; it's a powerful opportunity.

Rejection and **abandonment** in adulthood are situational. Many times they are about the preferences, needs, or circumstances of others and not about you. Your value isn't defined by who stays or who goes, who includes you or excludes you. The power to heal these wounds lies not in others but in your ability to step in as the adult villager—the **observer**—and offer comfort, reassurance, and **love** to your inner child.

Healing the Villagers of Abandonment and Rejection
True healing begins when you stop placing the responsibility for your inner child's safety on others. Partners, friends, or family can't quiet these villagers for you. It's your role and your responsibility to step in and say, "I will not leave you. I am here."

A Challenge to the Reader
Here's a practical way to start healing these wounded villagers:
1. Find a Photo: Locate a picture of yourself from a time when you felt **abandoned** or **vulnerable**—perhaps a childhood photo or one from a difficult period in your life.
2. Place It Somewhere Visible: Set this photo as the background on your phone or place it on your bathroom mirror—somewhere you'll see it daily.
3. Say Hello: Every time you see this photo, pause and say hello to your inner child. Remind them, II am here. I will never abandon you. We are in this together."
4. Be Consistent: Make this a daily practice. Over time, this simple act will strengthen your connection to your inner child, soothing the villagers of **abandonment** and **rejection**.

Practical Tools for Rejection:

When **rejection** arises, use these tools to reframe and heal:

1. Normalize **Rejection**:

    Rejection is a universal experience. Everyone faces it—often repeatedly—on their path to growth.

2. Reframe the Narrative:

    Instead of seeing **rejection** as a failure, view it as redirection. It's a sign that this opportunity, person, or path wasn't the right fit for you.

3. Reconnect with Yourself:

    When **rejection** triggers feelings of **inadequacy**, turn inward. Remind your inner child, *You are enough*, no matter what happens outside of you.

Moving Forward

Abandonment and **rejection** may still arise from time to time. Breakups, disagreements, and losses can trigger these wounds. Now, you have the tools to respond differently. You can recognize these experiences as echoes of the past and step in as the adult villager who will never abandon or reject your inner child.

The truth is, as long as you are here, you are never truly **abandoned**. The villagers of **abandonment** and **rejection** are not alone because you—the **observer**—are here to guide and protect them. It's not the responsibility of anyone else to fill that role. It's yours.

Every time you see that photo, remember this truth: "As long as I am here, breathing and present, my inner child is safe." Together, you can step out from under the porch, hand in hand, and rejoin the village.

So, let me ask you—who's hiding under the porch in your village? And what will you do to remind them that they're not alone?

Reflective Questions:
1. When was the last time you felt **rejected** or **abandoned**? How did your inner child react, and what could your adult self say to comfort and reassure them in that moment?
2. What belief about yourself do you think was shaped by an experience of **abandonment** or **rejection** in your childhood? How might that belief still be influencing your actions or relationships today?
3. How can you reframe a recent experience of **rejection** as redirection rather than a reflection of your worth? What opportunity might this **rejection** be pointing you toward instead?
4. What small, consistent practice can you adopt to remind your inner child that they are safe, **loved**, and never truly alone—regardless of external circumstances?

"Depression is your body saying, 'I don't want to be this character anymore. I don't want to hold up this avatar that you've created in the world.' It's your body's way of telling you that you need to stop being the character and start doing the things you truly want to do."

– Jim Carrey

CHAPTER 16

- Depression -
(When the Psyche Feels Heavy)

YOU are not **depressed**, you are observing a psyche that is **depressed**. **Depression**, like **anger**, is not who you are. It is a condition of the psyche —a state that you, as the **observer**, are present to witness. Just as you can experience **anger** without being consumed by it, you can experience **depression** without becoming it. This distinction is essential: slipping into **depression** is the same as slipping into **anger** or any other emotional state. The **observer**, as the conscious entity, does not slip. It remains strong, capable of seeing these emotional states rise and fall without being defined by them.

When **depression** takes hold, it is not a reflection of who you are at your core but a state within your psyche. The **observer**, standing at the cliff above the village, sees the weight that has settled over the villagers, the muted tones of the once-vibrant square, and the heaviness in the air. **Depression** is real, but it is not you. It is a temporary condition of the psyche, not the conscious self.

Depression in the Village

When the psyche falls into **depression**, the village reflects this state. The bustling square empties, the lively chatter quiets, and the villagers—your emotional parts—begin to retreat. Some sit silently at the edges of the village, weighed down by burdens they can't seem to put down. Others become sluggish, their movements slow and heavy. The villagers that normally bring **energy**, **joy**, and **curiosity** disappear into the fog, leaving the village unbalanced.

The Heavy Villagers

In the state of **depression**, certain villagers dominate the psyche, carrying immense weight. These villagers aren't bad or wrong; they are simply struggling under their own burdens, and their presence becomes **overwhelming** when the **observer** is not actively leading.

- *Grief*: This villager sits quietly, holding the weight of unacknowledged loss. **Grief** may mourn a **loved** one, a dream that didn't come true, or even the passing of time. Its heaviness comes from **love** that has no place to go, from stories that remain untold or unheard.
- *Shame*: The villager of **shame** whispers harsh words about **unworthiness** and **failure**. It retreats to the edges of the village, burdened by **self-doubt** and **fear of exposure**.

Shame feels heavy because it clings to old narratives, convinced they define the present.

- *Apathy*: **Apathy** lies still, unmoving. It sees no point in trying and no reason to hope. This villager's heaviness stems from **exhaustion**—the fatigue of unmet expectations and persistent disappointment.
- *Despair*: **Despair** stands alone, convinced that there is no path forward. It isolates itself, unwilling to engage with the other villagers. Its weight lies in its belief that change is impossible and that the fog will never lift.

Each of these villagers feel isolated and disconnected, amplifying their burdens. The **observer**, from its vantage point, sees this disconnection and recognizes the need to lead the villagers back into harmony.

The Role of the Observer

The **observer's** role in **depression** is not to fight or fix it but to witness and lead. The **observer**, as conscious **awareness**, remains distinct from the psyche's emotional states. It is not **depressed** but is present to see the **depression** unfold within the village. This detachment does not mean **indifference**; rather, it allows the **observer** to approach the situation with **curiosity** and **compassion**.

When the psyche is in **depression**, the **observer** can:
1. Acknowledge the State: The first step is to name what is happening. "The psyche is experiencing **depression**. The village is heavy." Naming the state separates it from the self, reducing the power it holds.
2. Engage with the Villagers: **Depression** often silences the villagers of **joy**, **curiosity**, and **connection** while amplifying the voices of **grief**, **shame**, and **despair**. The **observer** can reach out to these struggling villagers, asking, "What are you holding? What do you need from me?"
3. Invite Other Villagers: The **observer** can gently encourage the return of quieter villagers, like **hope** or **action**, to reintroduce balance. Small acts—taking a walk, practicing gratitude, or connecting with a loved one—can begin to shift the energy in the village.
4. Seek External Support: The **observer** can recognize when the village needs help from outside its borders. Reaching out to another **observer**, such as a therapist, friend, or mentor, can bring fresh perspective and guidance.

Depression as a Backpack of the Psyche
Depression often feels like an invisible backpack strapped to the psyche, weighing it down.

Each villager carries their own piece of this weight:
- **Grief** holds the stones of loss.
- **Shame** carries the bricks of self-doubt.
- **Apathy** lugs the dead weight of exhaustion.
- **Despair** clings to the anchor of hopelessness.

The **observer** doesn't carry this backpack, but it sees the villagers struggling under the load. The **observer's** job is not to take the burden away but to help the villagers lighten their loads— sometimes by simply sitting with them and listening, other times by taking small steps forward together.

Leading the Psyche Out of Depression
Depression is not a permanent state. Like a storm or a season, it will pass. The **observer's** job is to remain present through the storm, guiding the psyche even when the way forward isn't clear. This may mean embracing stillness when the villagers need rest, encouraging movement when they need momentum, or seeking connection when they feel alone.

Imagine the village in spring after a long, heavy winter. The snow melts, the sun returns, and the villagers begin to reemerge. **Joy** and **curiosity** dance in the square again. **Grief** and **shame**, though still present, find their place in the village center, where they can share their stories and lighten their loads.
The **observer** remains the constant through all of this—the leader who holds the staff, not as a symbol of **control** but as a beacon of leadership.

The Power of Awareness
The **observer** cannot be **depressed** because the **observer** is **awareness** itself. By recognizing **depression** as a state of the psyche rather than an **identity**, you can begin to create space for healing. **Depression** is not who you are—it is something you experience. And through the power of **awareness**, **compassion**, and **deliberate** action, the **observer** can guide the psyche back toward **balance**, one step at a time.

Who's talking in your village? And what do they need from you as their leader?

Reflective Questions:
1. When you feel the weight of **depression**, which villager do you think is speaking the loudest—**grief, shame, apathy**, or **despair**? What might they be trying to tell you, and how can you respond with compassion?
2. Reflect on a recent moment when your psyche felt heavy. How can you, as the **observer**, separate yourself from this state and acknowledge it without becoming it?
3. What small act of kindness or action could you invite into your village today to help **balance** the voices of **struggle** & **suffering** with the voices of **hope** and **connection**?
4. How might reaching out for external support, like speaking to a therapist, mentor, or trusted friend, help lighten the burdens of your struggling villagers.

*"You are not your job. You're not how much money you have in the bank. You're not the car you drive. You're not the contents of your wallet. You are not your f*ing khakis."*

– Tyler Durden

Chapter 17

- The Villager of Identity -
(Authenticity)

Identity is a powerful villager in your emotional village, often shaping how you perceive yourself and others. This villager whispers the *roles* we believe we must play: husband, wife, boyfriend, girlfriend, partner, brother, sister, mother, father. These *roles* are not inherently bad, but they are just *roles*—not who you are. And yet, many of us allow this villager to build our self-image entirely out of these labels, as if they define the core of our being.

The same happens in relationships. When we install someone in our lives as a "boyfriend," "girlfriend," or "partner," we risk seeing them as a pedestalized version of what we *imagine* those *roles* to mean. These labels come with baggage—cultural expectations, past experiences, societal norms—and when we unconsciously attach them to the people in our lives, we stop seeing who they truly are.

Take a moment to consider: the person in your life is not just a label. They are not "a boyfriend," "a girlfriend," or "a partner." They are *themselves*. They are a specific, complex individual you must learn uniquely, not generically. Similarly, you are not just a "husband," "wife," or "parent." You are uniquely *you*.

This issue extends far beyond relationships. Far too many times, I've had clients come to me and say, "I need to go find myself. I don't know who I am anymore." Once we start digging into what they mean, I find that their identity has become so entangled with their *roles*—wife, mother, teacher, doctor— and that they've forgotten who they are.

They've poured every ounce of themselves into these *roles*, living for their children, their spouse, or their career. And while these are meaningful parts of life, they are not *who you are*. Someone's profession might be teaching, but that is not their **identity**. Someone's role might be parenting, but that is not their essence. Who you are is the **observer** of the village, not the villagers themselves.

The problem is that for entirely too long, the **observer**—the true self—has been asleep. When the **observer** is unconscious, the villagers (emotions, *roles*, and thoughts) run the show. You've been showing up in life based solely on how these roles and feelings dictate. The **mother** villager cries, "You must sacrifice everything for your children!" The **teacher** villager demands, "You're only worthy if you have a successful career!" The **spouse** villager shouts, "Your happiness depends on keeping your partner happy!"

When this happens, the **observer** is drowned out by the noise. You stop asking, "Who am I?" and simply respond to the demands of the village. My goal is to wake you up.

Waking the Observer
You are not the mother. You are not the teacher. You are not the husband, the wife, the doctor, or the girlfriend. These are *roles* you play in your life. Important *roles*, yes, but they do not define the core of who you are. You are the **observer** of the village—the one who notices the *roles* and feelings as they arise.

When the **observer** awakens, it allows you to see clearly. You recognize the *roles* for what they are: responsibilities and connections you engage with, not **identities** you cling to. You stop letting the villagers of **identity** dictate your life and start showing up **authentically**.

This doesn't mean that you abandon your *roles*. It means you stop letting them define you. When the **observer** is awake, you can still be a mother or a teacher, but you do so with **awareness**. You can be a wife or a husband, but you bring your unique self to the role—not a generic template of what you think that *role* should be.

The Danger of Pedestalized Roles
This same principle applies in relationships. When we label someone as "partner" or "girlfriend," we often install them into a pedestalized

version of what we think that label **should** mean. Instead of seeing the person for who they are, we project our expectations onto them.

Take a moment to consider this: when you label someone as "boyfriend," you subconsciously bring in every idea you've ever had about how boyfriends **should** act. These ideas come from movies, culture, past relationships, or even your family. And when that person doesn't meet those unspoken expectations, resentment and turmoil brews.

The danger of these labels is that they erase the individual. You stop learning *this* person and instead start measuring them against your internal checklist.

To illustrate, let's return to Emma.

Emma and the Villager of Expectations

Emma was dating a man named James. At the beginning, their relationship felt promising—James called her his girlfriend, and they both leaned into the idea of building a life together. But over time, Emma started to notice subtle cracks in their connection.

James came from a culture where girlfriends were expected to behave in certain ways—quiet, accommodating, always ready to serve. Without ever realizing it, James had installed Emma into the mental slot labeled "Girlfriend" and began expecting her to act accordingly.

When Emma spent a weekend away with friends, James grew distant. "Why didn't you prioritize us?" he asked. When she made decisions independently, he seemed disappointed. "A girlfriend is supposed to include her boyfriend in everything," he'd say.

*But Emma wasn't just "a girlfriend." Emma was Emma. She showed **love** in her own way—by giving James thoughtful gifts, by supporting his goals, and by being fully present when they were together. Yet James couldn't see these things because he was measuring her against the template of what he believed a girlfriend **should** be.*

One evening, after another frustrating argument, Emma finally spoke up. "I don't think you see me," she said. "I think you see this idea of what a girlfriend is supposed to be, and when I don't fit into it, you get upset. But I'm not just your girlfriend. I'm Emma. And

Emma does things differently."

James was stunned. He hadn't realized how much his expectations were clouding his view of Emma as the unique individual that he was originally drawn to. He apologized, and for the first time, they began having honest conversations about who they truly were—not as roles, but as two people trying to get to know each other deeply.

Reclaiming the Observer

The villager of **identity** is loud, but it's not in charge. You are the **observer**—the one who notices the roles and the expectations without being controlled by them.

Ask yourself:
- Are you living as the **observer**, or are you asleep at the wheel while your *roles* run the show?
- Do you know who you are, or have you become lost in the labels others have assigned to you?
- Are you seeing the people in your life for who they truly are, or are you projecting your own expectations onto them?

When you wake up, you reclaim the ability to live **authentically**—not as a *role*, but as the unique individual that you truly are. And when you see others as individuals, not as labels, you create space for relationships to thrive.

The **observer** isn't confined by labels. The **observer** sees. And when you live as the **observer**, you bring your full self into every *role* you play—not as a mother, a teacher, or a partner, but as the awake, aware, **authentic** *you.*

Reflective Questions:
1. How have the *roles* you play in life—such as parent, partner, or professional—shaped your **identity**? Are these *roles* enhancing or limiting your sense of self?
2. Reflect on a close relationship in your life. Are you seeing this person for who they truly are, or are you measuring them against a set of expectations tied to their "*role*"?
3. When was the last time you felt lost or disconnected from yourself? How might reconnecting with the **observer**—the **authentic** you—help clarify your sense of **identity**?
4. What steps can you take to wake up the **observer** within you, allowing yourself to engage with life **authentically** rather than through the lens of *roles* or labels?

REMEMBER YOU ARE THE ONE WHO OBSERVES

Part 5:

Healing
&
Moving Forward

"I am not what happened to me. I am what I choose to become."

– Carl Jung

CHAPTER 18

- Trauma and Resilience -

(Understanding and Healing)

Trauma is a heavy word, one that carries the weight of **pain**, **fear**, and **loss**. It's not something any of us want to experience, but it's something many of us do. **Trauma** leaves an imprint on your village—a shadow that lingers, shaping how your villagers interact and react to the world around them. But **trauma** doesn't have to define your story. **Resilience** is the strength your village can build to grow beyond the **pain**, creating a new chapter from the ashes of the old.

Let's see how Emma faced her **trauma** and began her journey of **healing** and **resilience**.

Emma's Journey Through the Storm

Emma had always been close to her dad. He was her biggest supporter, her rock in difficult times. But when he passed away unexpectedly, her village was thrown into **chaos**. The villagers of **grief**, **anger**, and **guilt** each fought for **control**, **overwhelming** her **observer** and leaving her feeling **lost**.
For weeks, Emma felt like she was simply surviving, going through the motions of life. One day, while packing up her dad's belongings, she found a letter he'd written to her for her 18th birthday. In it, he wrote about how proud he was of her and how much he believed in her strength. As she read the letter, the villager of **hope** stirred quietly in the background—a voice Emma hadn't heard in a long time.
That moment became a turning point.
Emma realized that while she couldn't change what had happened, she could choose how she carried it forward. She began seeking support from friends, journaling about her emotions, and finding small ways to

honor her dad's memory. Over time, her village began to rebuild, stronger and more connected than before.

Understanding Trauma's Impact on Your Village

Trauma is any experience that **overwhelms** your ability to cope, leaving your villagers in a state of heightened alert. For some, it's a single event, like an accident or loss. For others, it's a series of smaller events that accumulate over time, like neglect or constant criticism. **Trauma** affects how your villagers respond to the world, often making them hyper-vigilant, withdrawn, or reactive.

Resilience is the process of helping your villagers recover from **trauma**. It's about creating **safety, connection,** and **purpose** in your village so the **observer** can regain **control**. This doesn't mean forgetting or minimizing the **trauma**—it means finding ways to move forward with **strength** and **grace**.

Remember, the **trauma** you experience is not who you are. It does not define you—it's a **painful** experience you went through, not the whole of your **identity**. In a way, you can view **trauma** as a form of accelerated learning. For instance, if a child burns their hand on a stove, it's a **traumatic** experience. But the accelerated learning is the knowledge that when the stove is on, it's hot, and it can hurt you. This is valuable information you didn't have before.

However, the next time you see a stove and feel triggered, remember that the trigger exists to remind your brain—not your heart—of the lesson. The **trauma** that happened is not happening now. What is occurring is that you've stored the disturbance inside yourself. When something in the present looks, feels, or smells like that past experience, it activates that old trigger. This is the moment to ask yourself, **"Who's talking?"** It could be the voice of your past self—the one who went through the **traumatic** event and is now afraid it might happen again.

I sometimes use this analogy with clients:

Imagine going to the grocery store and buying fresh fish for dinner. You prepare and enjoy the meal, tossing the leftover scraps and packaging into the trash. But instead of taking the trash outside, you leave it in your living room. Over time, the smell becomes unbearable, filling your space with an overwhelming stench.

That's how we often process experiences as humans. We take the valuable parts—the lessons, memories, or growth—and then hold onto the scraps, like **regret**, **guilt**, or **resentment**. Instead of letting them go, we keep them, stacking them in the corners of our minds, allowing them to pile up and fester. Eventually, this emotional clutter becomes pressurized, toxic, and overwhelming, leaving us feeling **anxious** and **stuck**.

The **observer's** role is to help us recognize what to keep and what to discard—enjoy the fish, but throw away the scraps, and make sure to take the trash out.

Tools for Healing and Building Resilience

1. The Safe Space Exercise:

    Visualize a safe place in your village where the **traumatized** villagers can rest and recover. This might be a quiet cozy cabin for **grief** or a guarded sanctuary for **fear**. Let them know they are protected and seen.

2. Naming and Reclaiming:

    Name the **trauma** and its impact on your village. For example, "This experience made my villager of **trust** afraid to connect with others." Acknowledging the impact is the first step toward reclaiming your power.

3. Create New Narratives:

    Rewrite the story your villagers are telling themselves. Instead of, "This happened to me, and I'll never recover," shift to, "This happened to me, but I'm finding ways to heal and grow."

Modern-Day Triggers for Trauma Responses

In today's world, **trauma** responses can be triggered by seemingly small events. A critical email might activate your villager of **insecurity**, reminding you of past failures. A news story might stir up the villager of **fear**, leaving you feeling **unsafe**. Recognizing these triggers and responding with **compassion** helps your village navigate the modern landscape with **resilience**.

A Funny Twist on Resilience

Imagine your villagers attending a **resilience** workshop. The villager of **despair** sits in the back, crossing their arms and muttering, "This won't work." Meanwhile, the villager of **hope** is leading the session, handing out tools like "deep breaths" and "positive affirmations." Your **observer** smiles, knowing that even the skeptics in your village can learn to heal in time.

Reflective Questions:
1. How has **trauma** affected your village, and which villagers are most impacted?
2. What small steps can you take to create **safety** and **connection** in your village?
3. How can you honor your past while focusing on building a **resilient** future?

Chapter 19

- Emotional Contracts and Expectations -

(The Invisible Agreements)

Emotional contracts are the unspoken agreements we carry in our relationships. These contracts outline how we believe others should behave, how we should be treated, or how life should unfold. The problem with these contracts is that they're often invisible—not just to others but sometimes to ourselves. When these expectations aren't met, the villagers of **resentment**, **disappointment**, and **frustration** rush in to take over.

Let's explore how Emma discovered her emotional contracts and learned to manage them effectively.

Emma's Unspoken Agreement

Emma had always been the one to organize family events. Every holiday, she would plan the menu, decorate the house, and make sure everyone had a great time. But last Thanksgiving, she was **overwhelmed** with work and decided to step back, assuming her sister, Claire, would take over. When Thanksgiving rolled around, Claire showed up empty-handed, expecting Emma to handle everything as usual. The villager of **resentment** immediately grabbed the staff. "She should have known to help! Why do I always have to do everything?"

Emma felt **unappreciated** and **taken for granted**.

Later that evening, Emma paused and asked herself, **"Who's talking?"** She realized that her resentment wasn't about Claire's behavior—it was about an unspoken emotional contract she had created. Emma had assumed that her sister would step in without ever discussing it. The expectation was invisible to Claire, which meant she couldn't possibly meet it.

*Emma decided to have an honest conversation with Claire, explaining how she felt and asking for help in the future. Claire was surprised, but willing to share the responsibilities.
By bringing the emotional contract into the open,
Emma was able to turn **resentment** into **collaboration**.*

Understanding Emotional Contracts

Emotional contracts often stem from unspoken preferences or assumptions. They can be as simple as expecting someone to remember your birthday or as complex as believing a partner should automatically know how to meet your emotional needs. The problem isn't the expectation itself—it's the lack of communication.

When these contracts go unmet, we feel **hurt**, **frustrated**, or **betrayed**. But more often than not, the other person isn't being malicious—they just don't know what's expected of them. The **observer's** role is to recognize these invisible agreements and decide whether to communicate them, let them go, or adjust your perspective.

Unmet expectations are something we've already discussed, and we know they lead to suffering. When we're dealing with relationships—whether with friends, family, lovers, or even the mailman—the most important thing to remember is that uncommunicated expectations are covert contracts that fast-track us to feelings of **contempt** for another person. But here's the catch: this is our problem, not theirs. No one knows what you expect in your own mind. Even when you communicate an expectation, don't just assume the outcome will match the preference you have. Once again, it's like playing cards. You can deal your card to me, and then it's my turn to play my cards back to you. You don't get to be **angry** if I don't play the card you wanted during this round—that's my choice, just like it's your choice to play the cards you select. The game only works if we actively communicate while playing. Otherwise, you're sitting in a room by yourself, getting **angry** at someone who isn't even there to play cards with you.

<u>Tools for Managing Emotional Contracts</u>
1. Name the Contract:
    Ask yourself: What am I expecting from this person or situation? Write it down to make the invisible visible.
2. Communicate Clearly:
    Share your expectations with others in a non-confrontational way. For example: "I've been feeling **overwhelmed** with holiday planning and would really appreciate your help next time."
3. Adjust or Release:
    If an emotional contract isn't realistic or fair, consider letting it go. Not every expectation needs to be fulfilled to maintain a healthy relationship.

Modern-Day Emotional Contracts

In the digital age, emotional contracts can extend to social media and other forms of communication. For instance, you might expect a friend to like your posts or respond to your texts immediately. When they don't, the villager of **insecurity** might whisper, "They don't care about you." Recognizing these modern contracts can help you step back and reassess whether your expectations are fair or necessary.

A Funny Twist on Emotional Contracts

Imagine your villagers negotiating emotional contracts with each other. The villager of **guilt** insists, "You should have known what I needed without me saying it!" Meanwhile, the villager of **logic** shakes their head and says, "Telepathy isn't a thing, Karen." Your **observer** steps in, gently reminding everyone that clear communication is key to avoiding unnecessary drama.

Reflective Questions:
1. What unspoken emotional contracts have you created in your relationships?
2. How can you communicate one of these contracts to someone in a way that strengthens your connection?
3. What's an expectation you can let go of to bring more **peace** to your village?

"Expectation is the root of all heartache."

– William Shakespeare

"Silence is golden, unless you have kids; then silence is just suspicious."

– Anonymous

Chapter 20

- When the Village Falls Silent -
(Navigating Emotional Numbness)

In the journey of **self-awareness**, there are moments when you ask, **"Who's talking?"** and are met with silence. This quietness can be unsettling, leaving you feeling disconnected or numb. Understanding this silence is crucial, as it often signals underlying emotional states that need attention.

Emma's Encounter with Silence

*Emma had been diligently practicing **self-awareness**, regularly checking in with her villagers. One evening, after a challenging day at work, she felt a heavy emptiness. She asked, **"Who's talking?"** but no villager responded. The silence was deafening, amplifying her sense of **isolation**. Confused, Emma sought guidance from a trusted friend. Through their conversation, she realized that her villagers were **overwhelmed**, leading to a state of emotional numbness. This **awareness** was the first step toward reconnecting with her emotions.*

Understanding Emotional Numbness

Emotional numbness is a state where you feel disconnected from your feelings and surroundings. It's as if your villagers have retreated into silence, leaving the village eerily quiet.

This numbness can result from:
- **Overwhelming Stress**: Prolonged exposure to stress can exhaust your emotional resources, leading to numbness.
- **Trauma**: Past traumatic experiences can cause your villagers to shut down as a protective mechanism.
- **Mental Health Conditions**: **Depression, anxiety,** and **PTSD** are often associated with **emotional numbness**.

- Medication Side Effects: Certain medications, like antidepressants, can lead to emotional blunting.

Recognizing that this silence is a response to underlying issues is essential. It's your villagers' way of coping, but prolonged numbness can hinder your ability to experience **joy**, **connection**, and **fulfillment**.

Strategies to Reconnect with Your Villagers

1. Mindful Awareness:
   Engage in practices of mindfulness to gently **observe** your internal state without judgment. This can help you become aware of the silence and its impact.
2. Physical Activity:
   Regular exercise can help "unfreeze" your emotions by releasing endorphins and reducing **stress**. Even a short walk can help make a difference.
3. Creative Expression:
   Engage in activities like drawing, writing, or playing music to provide an outlet for suppressed emotions.
4. Grounding Techniques:
   Use grounding exercises to reconnect with the present moment. This can include deep breathing, focusing on sensory experiences, or holding a comforting object.
5. Seek Professional Support:
   A mental health professional can help you explore the causes of your emotional numbness and develop strategies to address it.

A Lighthearted Perspective

Imagine your villagers have decided to take a silent retreat without informing you. They're all sitting in a circle, meditating quietly. Your **observer** walks in, puzzled, and says, "A little heads-up next time, folks!" This humorous scenario reminds us that sometimes, our inner world needs a break, and it's okay to seek understanding and reconnection.

Reflective Questions:
1. Have you experienced moments when your emotional village fell silent? What were the circumstances?
2. Which strategies resonate with you to help reconnect with your emotions?
3. How can you create a supportive environment for your villagers to feel safe expressing themselves again?

By acknowledging and addressing the silence within your village, you take a crucial step toward healing and emotional well-being. Remember, it's a journey, and seeking support along the way is a sign of strength.

"If you hear a voice within you say, 'You cannot paint,' then by all means paint, and that voice will be silenced."

– Vincent Van Gogh

CHAPTER 21

- The Villager of Self-Sabotage -
(Breaking the Cycle)

Deep within your village lives a villager who can be particularly tricky to deal with: the villager of **self-sabotage**. This villager doesn't want to hurt you on purpose, but its actions often seem to undermine your goals, relationships, or well-being. Whether it's procrastinating, avoiding responsibility, or pushing people away, **self-sabotage** comes from a misguided attempt to protect the village.

The **observer's** job is to recognize when this villager is running the show and understand why. By bringing **self-sabotage** into **awareness**, you can break the cycle and move forward with intention.

Emma's Struggle with Self-Sabotage
Emma had always dreamed of starting her own photography business. She had the talent, the equipment, and even a few clients lined up. But every time she sat down to create a business plan, she found herself scrolling social media, organizing her closet, or watching TV instead. One day, after another unproductive afternoon, Emma asked herself, **"Who's talking?"**
The villager of **self-sabotage** *stepped forward, muttering, "we don't fail, if we never try."*
Emma realized that this villager wasn't lazy or apathetic—it was **afraid**. *The fear of failure was so strong that it kept Emma stuck in place, convincing her to avoid trying at all.*
Once Emma identified the root of her **self-sabotage**, *she took small, manageable steps to confront it. Instead of focusing on the entire business plan, she set a timer for 20 minutes and worked on one section.*

*Over time, the villager of **self-sabotage** grew quieter as Emma built confidence in her abilities.*

Understanding Self-Sabotage
Self-sabotage often stems from unresolved fears, limiting beliefs, or unmet needs.

Common triggers include:
- **Fear of Failure**:
Avoiding effort to prevent the pain of falling short.
- **Fear of Success**:
Worrying that success will bring pressure or change.
- **Perfectionism**:
Believing that if something can't be done perfectly, it's not worth doing.
- **Low Self-Worth**:
Feeling undeserving of happiness, love, or success.

The villager of **self-sabotage** acts as a misguided protector. It tries to shield you from **disappointment**, **rejection**, or **discomfort**, but in doing so, it holds you back from growth and fulfillment.

Tools for Managing Self-Sabotage:
1. Name the Villager:
    When you notice **self-sabotaging** behavior, call it out: "This is the villager of **self- sabotage** trying to protect me. Naming it creates distance and reduces its power.
2. Ask "What's the **Fear**?":
    Identify the underlying **fear** driving the behavior. Are you afraid of **failure**? **Success**? **Criticism**? Understanding the **fear** helps you address it directly.
3. Take Small Steps:
    Break big tasks into smaller, less intimidating pieces. Each small success builds momentum and quiets the villager of **self-sabotage**.

4. Practice **Self-Compassion**:
> Remind yourself that **self-sabotage** doesn't make you weak or lazy—it's a natural response to **fear**. Approach it with **curiosity** and **kindness** rather than **judgment**.

5. Set Clear Intentions:
> Write down your goals and the steps needed to achieve them. Clarity helps counteract the confusion and avoidance that **self-sabotage** thrives on.

Modern-Day Self-Sabotage

In today's world, **self-sabotage** often disguises itself as busyness or distraction.Social media, endless to-do lists, and fear of missing out can all feed the villager of **self-sabotage**, keeping you from focusing on what truly matters. Recognizing these patterns is the first step toward reclaiming your time and energy.

Deepening the Understanding of Self-Sabotage and Reframing Disorders

Self-sabotage and behaviors often labeled as "disorders" are frequently misunderstood and unfairly internalized as defects. We live in a world that rewards certain traits—efficiency, linear progress, and constant achievement. But what happens when your natural instincts, abilities, or ways of being don't align with the modern environment? This mismatch doesn't mean you're broken; it means the system wasn't designed with your unique strengths in mind.

Take ADHD, for example. It's often labeled as a "disorder" because it doesn't fit the mold of our industrialized, capitalistic systems that prioritize focus, sustained productivity, and measurable outcomes. However, ADHD isn't inherently a problem—it's a set of traits that shine in different contexts, such as environments requiring adaptability, creativity, or rapid problem-solving. People with attention deficits tend to notice details or patterns others might miss. This attentiveness to novelty can help them identify opportunities and insights in environments where attention to change is critical. When viewed through the lens of mismatched environments, ADHD—and self-sabotage—are not personal failings but reflections of a system designed to highlight certain strengths while neglecting others.

To better understand this, imagine a porcupine in a world designed for cheetahs. The porcupine isn't fast, sleek, or built for speed, but that doesn't make it inadequate or have a "disorder". Its slow pace, spikes, and deliberate movement make perfect sense in an ecosystem where survival doesn't depend on speed. Similarly, a snake isn't built for endurance, but its venom is a powerful strength. If you judged the porcupine or snake by a cheetah standards, they'd always come up short, but that doesn't mean they're broken or disordered. It means their value lies in thriving within the ecosystem suited to their unique traits.

In the same way, self-sabotage often emerges when your natural instincts are at odds with societal expectations. The villager of self-sabotage doesn't exist to ruin your life; it's a misguided protector. It may whisper, "Why even try? You'll never fit in here." Or it might convince you that because you don't thrive in structured systems, you're fundamentally flawed. But this villager isn't your enemy—it's scared. It fears failure, rejection, or being judged by a world that only celebrates certain ways of thinking and being.

This doesn't mean self-sabotage—or traits labeled as disorders—should be excused or ignored. It means they should be understood. Self-sabotage thrives in environments where your strengths aren't celebrated, but the goal isn't to silence this villager. The goal is to work with it. When Emma's villager of self-sabotage told her, "We don't fail if we never try," it wasn't trying to destroy her dreams of becoming a photographer. It was trying to shield her from the pain of judgment. By recognizing this, Emma was able to respond with compassion, saying, "I see you, but we're going to try anyway." She started small, not to dismiss her villager's concerns, but to gently show it that trying wasn't as scary as it seemed.

The same applies to disorders like ADHD. Just as the porcupine isn't inadequate for lacking speed, individuals with ADHD—or other traits that don't align with societal norms—aren't broken. They're simply navigating an environment that is not built to celebrate their strengths. This is where the real responsibility lies: recognizing your unique traits and finding ways to thrive in or adapt to the environment, rather than allowing self-sabotage or societal labels to define you.

A New Perspective on Responsibility

It's important to acknowledge that while the environment may not be in your control, how you respond to it is your responsibility. The most dangerous trap of self-sabotage—and the way disorders are framed—is the belief that because the world isn't built for you, you're doomed to fail. This victim mindset is like slipping into a downward spiral of a toilet bowl, robbing you of agency and hope.

Instead of asking, "What's wrong with me?" ask, "What kind of environment allows me to thrive?" This shift empowers you to lean into your strengths, seek out spaces that celebrate your unique traits, and advocate for systems that value diversity in thinking and being. By reframing self-sabotage and disorders as reflections of mismatched environments, you can move from feeling defective to feeling empowered. You are not broken—you're different. And that difference is your power.

By understanding the villager of self-sabotage and questioning the labels society places on your unique traits, you can transform these perceived roadblocks into opportunities for growth. Self-sabotage isn't your enemy, and neither are the traits labeled as disorders. They're both guides, helping you recognize the environments where you're most likely to succeed. When you work with them, instead of against them, you can create a life that celebrates who you truly are.

A Funny Twist on Self-Sabotage

Imagine your villager of **self-sabotage** as a clumsy but well-meaning assistant. They knock over your coffee while saying, "I thought you needed a break! " or rearrange your desk, insisting, "You can't work in this chaos!" Your **observer** steps in, gently but firmly saying, "Thank you, but I've got this."

Reflective Questions
1. What **self-sabotaging** behaviors do you notice in your own life?
2. What **fears** or beliefs might be driving these behaviors?
3. How can you take small steps to counteract **self-sabotage** and move toward your goals?
4. How have societal expectations made you feel like you don't "fit"?
5. In what ways can you reframe self-sabotaging behaviors or traits labeled as disorders as attempts to protect or adapt?
6. What unique strengths do you bring to your life that might not be celebrated by traditional systems?
7. How can you begin to adapt to environments where your strengths shine, rather than trying to force yourself into systems that don't align with your abilities?

"Do not dwell in the past, do not dream of the future, concentrate the mind on the present moment."

– Buddha

CHAPTER 22

- Being Open in the Moment -
(Letting Go of Control)

At its core, life revolves around two questions:
1. "I liked that, how do I get more of it?"
2. "I didn't like that, how do I avoid it?"

These questions shape much of what we do. They guide our goals, influence our relationships, and dictate our habits. But the problem isn't the questions themselves—it's where we ask them from. Too often, these questions are tied to the past or the future, keeping us trapped in a cycle of attachment, expectation, and **control**.

What if the real purpose of life isn't to **control** it but to stay open in the moment and experience it fully?

The present moment is the only time we truly have. When we shift our focus from **controlling** the outcomes of life to opening ourselves to what naturally unfolds, we free ourselves from the **stress** of unmet expectations and the weight of the past. Let's explore how we can break free from this cycle and live in the now.

Emma's Realization

Emma had always been a planner.
She meticulously scheduled every aspect of her life, believing that ***controlling*** *her time would make her happy. But no matter how much she planned, life had a way of throwing unexpected curveballs—*
an argument with a friend, a work project that went off track,
a vacation that didn't live up to her hopes.
One evening, after a particularly stressful day, Emma sat down and reflected on her frustration.

She realized her mind was stuck in two places:
The past, replaying what had gone wrong.
The future, imagining how she could prevent it from happening again.
In that moment, Emma asked herself, "What if I just stopped?"
*What if she let go of the need to **control** and simply experienced the present moment? She decided to try. That night, Emma put her phone down, took a walk, and focused on the sound of her footsteps, the feel of the breeze, and the colors of the sunset.*
For the first time in a long time, she felt at peace.

The Cycle of Attachment and Avoidance

The two core questions—"How do I get more of what I enjoy?" and "How do I avoid what I don't" —are reasonable, but they often pull us away from the present.

Here's how:
- Attachment to the Past: We hold onto things we've enjoyed, **fearing** they'll never come again, or replay painful moments, hoping to rewrite or understand them.
- Resistance to the Future: We try to **control** outcomes, avoiding uncertainty, or chase after idealized versions of our lives that don't exist.

Both are rooted in the illusion that we can **control** life. But the truth is, life can't be **controlled**—it can only be lived. The **observer's** role is to recognize this pattern and redirect your focus to the present moment.

Why Presence is the Key

The present is where life happens. It's where you feel the warmth of the sun on your skin, laugh with a friend, or take a deep breath after a long day. The past is gone, and the future hasn't yet arrived. When you stop trying to **control** what's outside your reach, you create space to experience life fully.

Questions to Reflect On:
- What would happen if you let go of the need to get more or avoid less?
- How can you engage more deeply with the moment in front of you?
- What **joy** might you discover by simply being?

Tools for Living in the Present:
1. Let Go of Attachments:
    Recognize when you're clinging to past joys or resisting future outcomes. Ask yourself, "What can I release to feel lighter right now?"
2. Embrace Preferences, Not Demands:
    Preferences are natural, but attaching to expected outcomes creates suffering. Remind yourself, "I'd like this to happen, but it's okay if it doesn't."
3. Practice Mindfulness:
    Ground yourself in the moment by focusing on your senses. What can you see, hear, touch, or smell right now?
4. Use the Question **"Who's Talking?"**:
    When you feel uneasy or overwhelmed, ask which villager is trying to **control** the narrative. Invite them to step back and let the **observer** lead.

A New Purpose: Experiencing Life

Many people search for the meaning of life, but what if the purpose is simpler than we think? What if the purpose of life is simply to experience it? To be present for its joys and challenges, its beauty and chaos, without needing to **control** or judge it.

When you focus on experiencing life instead of **controlling** it, everything shifts. You begin to notice the little things—a kind smile, a beautiful sunset, the way rain sounds on the roof. These moments don't require anything from you but your presence.

A Funny Twist on Control

Imagine your villagers at a board meeting, trying to plan every detail of your life. The villager of **control** yells, "We need a five-year plan!" While the villager of **anxiety** scribbles worst-case scenarios on a whiteboard. Your **observer** steps in with a cup of tea, saying, "How about we focus on enjoying this meeting instead?"

Reflective Questions:
1. How often do you find yourself clinging to the past or trying to **control** the future?
2. What small step can you take to bring more presence into your daily life?
3. How would your life change if you let go of the need to **control** it and simply experienced it instead?

Chapter 23

- The Power of Grief -
(Love with No Place to Go)

Grief is one of the most profound emotions we can experience. It's the echo of **love** when the object of that **love** is no longer present. It feels like **love** with no place to go—a deep yearning for connection, mixed with the painful reality of absence.

Grief reminds us of what we've lost, but it also reveals the depth of our capacity to **love**. While it's a force that can feel **overwhelming**, **grief** has a transformative power when embraced with understanding and compassion.

Emma's Journey Through Grief

Emma's grandmother had been her rock—a constant source of wisdom, warmth, and unconditional love. When her grandmother passed away, Emma felt like a part of her village had been wiped out. The villager of **sorrow** *held the staff, walking silently through the streets, while the villager of* **anger** *shouted,*
"Why did this happen? It's not fair!"
For weeks, Emma avoided her feelings, throwing herself into work and distractions. But one evening, as she sorted through her grandmother's belongings, the **grief** *overwhelmed her. She sat on the floor, holding an old photo, and finally allowed herself to feel the full weight of her loss. In that moment, Emma realized* **grief** *wasn't something to escape—it was a reflection of how much her grandmother meant to her. By acknowledging her* **pain***, she began to transform her* **grief** *into gratitude for the memories they had shared.*

Grief as Love with No Place to Go

To me, **grief** seems like **love** with no place to go. When you lose someone, you can no longer gift them your **love**. You cannot give this same **love** to someone else because it isn't theirs to receive, and you can't simply leave it behind because it's too precious.

Instead, we carry this **grief** with us like a suitcase labeled **Love**. And every once in a while, that suitcase opens up, spilling its contents everywhere. As we cry and gather up those pieces, we are reminded of how much that person meant to us and how deeply we still care. They are no longer here to receive our **love**, so we pack it all back into the suitcase, clip it shut, stand tall, and carry forward in the face of this adversity.

This is what it means to be human. **Grief** is not just **pain**—it's a testament to **love**, **resilience**, and the capacity to **endure** even when carrying the heaviest of loads.

The Dual Nature of Grief

Grief is often described as a journey, and it's one that looks different for everyone. At its core, grief serves two purposes:

1. To Honor What Was: **Grief** connects us to the **love** and meaning we found in someone or something we've **lost**.
2. To Transform What Is: **Grief** can be a catalyst for growth, helping us find new ways to carry the **love** we've lost and integrate it into our lives.

There are two main types of **grief** to consider:

1. **Death Grief**: This occurs when someone we **love** is gone forever. The **love** we carry for them has no physical place to land, which creates a profound sense of longing and emptiness.
2. **Ambiguous Grief**: This arises when someone is still present but fundamentally changed. They look like them, they sounds like

them, but it's no longer them — through illness, estrangement, or life transitions. This could be seen in areas like dementia, divorce or gender transitions. It's the **grief** of losing who they once were to you while they're still alive.

Both forms of **grief** challenge us to let go of what we cannot **control** while holding onto the **love** that remains.

The Weight of Unprocessed Grief

Grief, when unacknowledged, doesn't disappear—it lingers in the shadows of your village, influencing your thoughts and actions. The villagers of **avoidance** and **numbness** often step in, trying to protect you from the **pain**, but their efforts can lead to feelings of disconnection or unresolved sorrow.

Imagine your **grief** as a heavy box. You've unpacked some of its contents, but instead of discarding the box, you keep it in your bedroom, adding it to a pile of other emotional boxes. Over time, the weight grows, and the space becomes cluttered. Processing **grief** means unpacking the box, keeping the lessons and **love** inside, and finding a way to honor it without letting the emotional boxes take over your life.

Tools for Navigating Grief :
1. Name the Villager of **Grief**:
    Acknowledge the presence of **grief** in your village. Naming allows you to see it as a part of you, not the entirety of who you are.
2. Allow Yourself to Feel:
    Grief demands to be felt. Suppressing it only prolongs its hold over you. Set aside time to sit with your feelings, whether through journaling, meditation, or simply being present with your emotions.

3. Honor the Love Behind the **Grief**:
    Create a ritual or space to honor what you've lost—a photo, a letter, or a moment of reflection. Let this practice remind you of the **love** that the **grief** represents.
4. Seek Connection:
    Grief can feel **isolating**, but sharing your experience with trusted friends, family, or a support group can provide comfort and perspective.
5. Find Meaning in the **Pain**:
    Over time, explore how your **grief** can transform into action—whether through helping others, creating something meaningful, or simply living in a way that honors what you've lost.

The Transformative Power of Grief

Grief changes you, but it doesn't have to break you. It's a force that can open your heart, deepen your empathy, and strengthen your connection to life's fragility and beauty. By embracing **grief** as part of your journey, you allow yourself to grow through the **pain**, rather than being consumed by it.

A Funny Twist on Grief

Imagine your villagers holding a memorial for something you've lost. The villager of **sorrow** gives a heartfelt somber speech, while the villager of **anger** stomps around shouting, "This is ridiculous!" Your **observer** steps in, handing everyone tissues and saying, "Let's remember the good times too." Slowly, the villagers come together, sharing stories and laughter through their tears.

The following addition is the heart of this book, the place where the entire concept of the village began. To truly do justice to the ideas here, I need to be vulnerable for a moment—because this book could never have been written without including what I'm about to share.

The Multidimensional Loss of Grief

When we lose someone we **love**, it is never just one person we lose. **Grief** is not as simple as mourning a singular role—it is the unbearable realization that many dimensions of connection have vanished all at once. Each relationship we have with someone is a web of roles, spanning generations, emotions, and different parts of ourselves. When that web collapses, it leaves holes in the fabric of our inner world that seem impossible to mend.

When I lost my wife, I didn't just lose her. I lost a mother, a daughter, a sister, and a lover. And when I lost my adopted father, I lost him in three profound ways: as a father, as a son, and as a friend. These weren't just symbolic roles—they were deeply lived, real connections, tied to specific versions of me and the different parts of them. **Grief**, in these moments, felt like the destruction of entire relationships and pieces of myself that were uniquely tied to the people I **loved**.

The Many Roles We Play

Every significant relationship is a constellation of roles. The people we **love** are never just one thing to us. They are caretakers, confidants, companions, and even dependents. When they're gone, we don't just mourn the person—we mourn the countless ways they touched our lives and the versions of ourselves that existed only in connection to them.

Losing My Wife
When I lost my wife, the devastation was profound because she was so many things to me:
- A Mother: In my moments of weakness, she cared for me, nurtured me, and offered stability when I couldn't find it within myself.
- A Daughter: In her moments of vulnerability, I stepped in to protect her, to parent her, to be the strength she sometimes needed.
- A Sister: Our inner children played together in ways that only we understood. We laughed, shared secrets, and cared for each other like siblings at heart.
- A Lover: She was my partner, my companion, my confidant, and the anchor of my adult life.

When I lost her, I didn't lose one person—I lost four. Each of these *roles* was tied to a different part of me: the adult me, the inner child me, the protector me. Each connection vanished, leaving an emptiness that felt infinite.

Losing My Adopted Father
Losing my father was another monumental loss, one that felt as heavy and complex as losing my wife, though in a different way. I am the one who found him after he took his own life—a moment in time that changed me forever. In that instant, I lost him in three distinct ways:
- As a Father: He was the man who raised me, who shaped my understanding of what it means to be cared for. Losing him was losing the person who had always been there, even in his imperfection, as a guiding figure in my life.
- As a Son: In his later years, our roles reversed, and I became his caretaker. I parented him, stepping in when he could no longer care for himself. Losing him in this way was like losing a child—a role reversal that left me grieving the love I could no longer give.
- As a Friend: My father wasn't just a parent—he was my confidant, my equal in many ways. He was someone I could talk to, joke with, and rely on as a companion in life. His absence left a void that no one else could fill.

When he died, I didn't just lose one man—I lost the father who guided me, the child I cared for, and the friend who stood by me. **Grief** struck three times over, and I was left with the haunting pain of unexpressed **love**, knowing there were things I would never get to say or do with him again.

The Layered Weight of Grief

This is the true weight of **grief**: when someone we **love** is gone, we lose not just the person but all the *roles* they played in our lives. We lose the parent, the child, the friend, the confidant, and the partner. We lose the adult version of them, the child version of them, and the ways they connected with the adult and child versions of us. These layered losses are what make **grief** feel so heavy, so infinite.

Grief isn't just about missing someone—it's about losing the pieces of ourselves that existed only in connection to them. It's about realizing that no one will ever play those exact roles again, and that some versions of ourselves will never be seen, cared for, or understood in the same way.

The Catastrophic Loss of Connection

When I lost my wife and my father, I didn't just lose people—I lost entire ecosystems of **connection**, **love**, and **identity**. With my wife, I lost the adult who grounded me, the child I nurtured, the friend I laughed with, and the lover I shared my life with. With my father, I lost the man who raised me, the child I cared for, and the friend who could never be replaced.

Grief is so incredibly catastrophic because it forces us to confront not just the absence of one person, but the collapse of every relationship they embodied in our lives. It is the loss of countless connections, countless *roles*, and countless moments that will never happen again.

Moving Through the Void
Healing from such a loss doesn't mean erasing the pain or replacing the *roles* that were lost. It means honoring the magnitude of the **grief** and learning to rebuild your village around it. It means recognizing that while the people we **love** may be gone, the impact they had on our lives remains. The *roles* they played may no longer exist in the same way, but the **love** and lessons they gave us continue to shape who we are.

When we lose someone significant, we lose pieces of ourselves—but we also gain the opportunity to carry their memory forward, to let their influence live on in how we **love**, care, and connect with others. **Grief** is a reminder of how deeply we've **loved**, and how profoundly we've been **loved** in return.

Closing Thoughts
Grief is not a singular loss. It is the loss of many *roles*, many relationships, and many parts of ourselves. To truly heal, we must allow ourselves to feel the full weight of what we've lost while also honoring the **love** that remains. When I think about my wife and my father, I see the ways they shaped me, the ways they cared for me, and the ways I cared for them. I carry those connections with me, even as I mourn the ones that are gone.

*- To grieve deeply
is to have loved deeply.
And while the loss is immeasurable,
so too is the love that lingers. -
With all my love,*

Part 6:

Mastery & Leadership

"The nearer a man comes to a calm mind, the closer he is to strength."

– Marcus Aurelius

CHAPTER 24

- Calm Is Contagious -
(Leadership Through Emotional Regulation)

There's an old military saying: **Calm** is **contagious**. In moments of **chaos** or high **stress**, the person who remains **calm** becomes the anchor for everyone else. People instinctively look to the **calmest** person in the room for direction, guidance, and reassurance. This principle doesn't just apply to the battlefield—it's true in families, friendships, workplaces, and any environment where emotions run high.

When your villagers are in a state of **chaos**—**fear** running one way, **anger** stomping another, and **panic** screaming in the corner—it's your **observer's** job to take the staff and restore order. The more you practice emotional regulation, the more contagious your **calm** becomes. Let's see how Emma applied this principle in her life.

Emma's Crisis of Calm

Emma was in charge of organizing a major charity event for her workplace. The day of the event, everything seemed to go wrong. The caterer arrived late, the sound system malfunctioned, and a key speaker canceled last minute. As the **chaos** *unfolded, Emma's coworkers started panicking, their villagers of* **anxiety** *running wild.* Emma could feel her own villager of **overwhelm** grabbing for the staff. But instead of letting it take over, she paused, took a deep breath, and asked herself, **"Who's talking?"** She realized that if she allowed her own **chaos** to spread, it would only make things worse. Emma knew that she needed to lead by example. She stepped up, **calmly** delegating tasks to her team and reassuring them that they could handle the setbacks. Her **calm** demeanor inspired others to take action instead of spiraling into **stress**. By the time the *event started, everything had fallen into place. Emma's ability to stay composed didn't just save the day—it earned her the respect and admiration of her coworkers.*

The Power of Emotional Regulation
Your emotional state influences those around you more than you realize. When you remain **calm** in a high-**stress** situation, you create a ripple effect, helping others feel more grounded and capable. On the other hand, if you let your villagers of **fear** or **frustration** take **control**, that energy spreads just as quickly.
Emotional regulation doesn't mean suppressing your feelings or pretending everything is fine. It means acknowledging your villagers, listening to their concerns, and choosing how to respond. This deliberate approach allows you to lead your village—and others—with clarity and confidence.

Tools for Staying Calm Under Pressure
1. Box Breathing:
    This military technique is simple but powerful: breathe in for 4 seconds, hold for 4 seconds, breathe out for 4 seconds, and hold again for 4 seconds. Repeat until you feel centered and **calm**.
2. Name the Feeling:
    Identify the dominant villager in the moment. Saying, "This is **anxiety** talking," or "This is **frustration**," helps you create distance from the emotion and take back **control**.
3. Focus on What You Can **Control**:
    In any crisis, there are things you can influence and things you can't. Direct your energy toward what's within your power to change, and let go of the rest.

Modern-Day Applications of Calm
In today's fast-paced world, staying **calm** can feel like a superpower. From navigating difficult conversations to dealing with unexpected

challenges, your ability to regulate your emotions sets the tone for everyone around you. Whether it's a family argument, a workplace emergency, or even a long line at the grocery store, your calmness can transform the situation.

A Funny Twist on Calm

Imagine your villagers in a full-blown panic. The villager of **fear** is running in circles, screaming, "We're doomed!" while the villager of **frustration** throws their hands in the air, shouting, "This is a disaster!" Your **observer** walks in calmly, holding a cup of tea, and says, "Let's all take a breath, shall we?" Slowly, the villagers settle down, realizing that the world hasn't ended after all.

Reflective Questions:

1. Think of a recent situation where staying **calm** made a difference. How did it impact the people around you?
2. What triggers tend to disrupt your **calm**, and how can you prepare for them?
3. How can you practice being the **calm** anchor in your relationships and community?

"To forgive is to set a prisoner free and discover that the prisoner was you."

– Lewis B. Smedes

Chapter 25

- The Villager of Forgiveness -
(Letting Go of the Past)

The villager of **forgiveness** often stands quietly in the background, overshadowed by louder villagers like **resentment**, **anger**, and **guilt**. But when given the staff, **forgiveness** has the power to transform the village. It is not about forgetting or excusing past wrongs—it's about releasing the heavy emotional burdens that keep us tethered to the past.

Forgiveness is as much a gift to ourselves as it is to others. It is the process of untangling ourselves from the **pain** and freeing up energy to live fully in the present. At its core, **forgiveness** is the ultimate act of **self-compassion** and **liberation**.

Forgiveness and Karma: A New Perspective
Many people view karma as a cosmic system of justice—what someone does will eventually come back to them. But what if karma isn't external at all? What if karma is internal—the things we store from the past that come back to haunt us in the future?

Think of it this way: every unresolved hurt, grudge, or regret you carry is like a stone in a backpack. Over time, the weight becomes unbearable, making it harder to move forward. This is your karma—your unprocessed **pain** and unresolved emotions.

Forgiving yourself and others is how you begin to lighten the load. It's not about excusing bad behavior or pretending the hurt didn't happen. It's about acknowledging the **pain**, processing it, and choosing to set it down so that it doesn't shape your future.

Emma's Story of Forgiveness

*Emma had been carrying a grudge against her brother for years. He had borrowed money during a tough time and never paid her back, even after getting back on his feet. Every time she thought about him, the villager of **resentment** shouted, "He owes us!"*

The grudge seeped into every interaction they had, creating a wall between them.

*One day, Emma realized how much energy she was pouring into this **resentment**. She asked herself, "Who's really suffering here?" The villager of **forgiveness** stepped forward and gently said,*

"You can let this go.
You don't need to carry this anymore."

*Emma decided to **forgive** her brother—not because he deserved it, but because she deserved peace. She acknowledged her **hurt**, released her expectation of repayment, and chose to move forward. By letting go, Emma felt lighter, freer, and more connected to her brother than she had in years.*

The Dual Act of Forgiveness

Forgiveness comes in two forms:
1. Forgiving Others: Letting go of the **pain** others have caused you, not for their sake, but for your own peace.
2. Forgiving Yourself: Releasing **guilt** or **shame** for your own mistakes and choices, recognizing that you're human and deserve **compassion**.

Both forms of **forgiveness** are essential for emotional freedom. Holding onto **anger** or **resentment** is like drinking poison and expecting someone else to suffer—However, it only harms you.

Tools for Practicing Forgiveness:

1. Acknowledge the **Pain**:
   Name the villager behind your **hurt**—whether it's **resentment**, **guilt**, or **shame**. Understanding its role helps you address it with **compassion**.

2. Reframe the Narrative:
   Instead of focusing on the harm caused, ask yourself, "What can I learn from this?" Shifting your perspective can transform **pain** into growth.

3. Release the Debt:
   Let go of the expectation that the person who hurt you **should** make it right. **Forgiveness** is about freeing yourself, not waiting for someone else to act.

4. Write a Letter:
   Write a letter to the person you're **forgiving**, expressing your feelings. You don't have to send it—just the act of writing can be healing.

5. Forgive in Layers:
   Forgiveness is a process, not a one-time act. Be patient with yourself and others as you work through the layers of pain.

Karma and Forgiveness

If karma is the emotional baggage we carry, **forgiveness** is how we unpack it. By releasing grudges and **guilt**, we break the cycle of karma, preventing the past from shaping our future.

Imagine your village as a garden. Each grudge or unresolved **pain** is a weed, choking the life out of the flowers. **Forgiveness** is the act of pulling those weeds, making space for new growth. It doesn't erase the fact that the weeds were there and some buried seed may bring them back, but it allows the garden to begin to thrive again.

A Funny Twist on Forgiveness

Picture the villager of **forgiveness** in your village, walking around with a broom and dustpan. They sweep up the mess left by **resentment** and **guilt**, humming a cheerful tune. Meanwhile, the villager of **anger** grumbles, "Do we really have to clean this up?" **Forgiveness** replies, "Yes, because I'm tired of tripping over it!"

Reflective Questions:
1. What grudges or regrets are you carrying that feel like stones in your backpack?
2. How would it feel to set those stones down and walk forward without them?
3. What's one step you can take today to **forgive** yourself or someone else?

CHAPTER 26

- Healing -
(Time Doesn't Heal All Wounds)

You've likely heard the saying, "Time heals all wounds." It's a comforting phrase, often repeated to soothe someone in **pain**. But what if I told you that time doesn't heal wounds—ever? Time alone has never healed a single broken bone, mended a single heart, or resolved a single **trauma**. Healing is not something that happens because days, months, or years pass. It happens because of active work beneath the surface, whether you see it or not.

At best, time allows **pain** to lay dormant. It may seem like it's gone, but the truth is, it's merely waiting for the right moment—a trigger—to resurface. Triggers bring unresolved **pain** rushing back into focus, reminding you of the work left undone. Emotional wounds, like physical ones, don't disappear just because you've moved forward. If they're not addressed, they remain fractures in your psyche, influencing your life in subtle, often destructive ways. Let's take a closer look at why this is true, starting with the body's approach to healing.

How a Bone Heals
When a bone breaks, time doesn't heal it—your body does. The process begins the moment the fracture occurs, initiating a series of active and deliberate steps. Without these steps, the bone remains broken, regardless of how much time passes.

Here's how the body actively heals:

1. Hematoma Formation:
Within hours, blood vessels around the fracture rupture, forming a blood clot (hematoma). This clot stabilizes the area and provides the foundation for healing to begin.

2. Soft Callus Formation:
Over the next few days, specialized cells (fibroblasts and chondroblasts) create a soft callus—a bridge of tissue connecting the broken ends. While not yet strong, this structure is critical to the repair process.

3. Hard Callus Formation:
Bone-forming cells (osteoblasts) replace the soft callus with new bone. This hard callus strengthens the fracture site, preparing it to bear weight again.

4. Bone Remodeling:
Over weeks or months, the bone reshapes itself into its original form, becoming as strong—or stronger—than before the fracture.

The body is constantly working to heal the break. Time provides the space for these processes to unfold, but it's the active, invisible work of the body that repairs the damage.

The Emotional Parallel

Emotional wounds operate the same way. **Trauma** creates fractures in your psyche—breaks that disrupt your sense of **safety**, **worth**, or **connection**. Time doesn't heal these fractures any more than it heals a broken bone. At best, it allows the **pain** to fade into the background, but without active engagement, the wound remains.

When triggered, the unresolved trauma resurfaces, often with the same intensity as when it first occurred. This is why someone can seem fine for years, only to be **overwhelmed** by a memory, a comment, or an experience that pulls them back into their **pain**. Time alone doesn't heal emotional wounds—it just delays their impact.

Stored Disturbances in Your Village

Unhealed **trauma** lingers as a stored disturbance in your village. Certain villagers—**fear, grief, shame**—carry the weight of these unresolved wounds, affecting the harmony of your inner world. These disturbances don't resolve themselves; they influence your thoughts, behaviors, and relationships until actively addressed.

- **Fear** whispers, Don't trust anyone—it's safer this way.
- **Grief** clutches tightly to loss, convinced that letting go means forgetting.
- **Shame** insists, You're not worthy of **love** or belonging.

Left unchecked, these villagers influence your life in ways you may not even realize. They shape your reactions, hold you back from growth, and create patterns that repeat until the root cause is healed.

The Observer's Role in Healing

Healing isn't about waiting for time to pass. It's about stepping into your role as the **observer** and actively engaging with the wounded villagers in your psyche. Just as your body works behind the scenes to heal a broken bone, you must work behind the scenes to heal your emotional wounds.

The **observer's** role is to approach each wounded villager with **curiosity** and **compassion**, listening to their stories and helping them release their burdens. Healing happens when you bring **awareness** to what was hidden and guide your village toward integration.

Active Healing: Villager to Villager

Each wounded villager requires a unique approach:

1. **Grief**:

This villager needs reassurance that letting go doesn't mean forgetting. **Grief** holds onto love that has no place to go. The

observer can guide this villager toward honoring the loss while finding new ways to let love flow.

2. **Shame**:
Shame carries the story of unworthiness. The **observer** must gently challenge this narrative, reminding **shame**: You are not defined by your mistakes. You are worthy as you are.

3. **Fear**:
Fear clings to **safety**, believing it's protecting you. The **observer** can acknowledge this intention while guiding **fear** toward trust in the present moment.

Letting Go as an Active Process

Letting go is often portrayed as passive—something you simply decide to do. But true, letting go is an active, repetitive process. It requires conscious effort to confront the narrative, speak to the villager holding onto the **pain**, and choose to release it again and again.

1. Awareness: Recognize when a **trauma**-based narrative arises.
2. Engagement: Speak to the villager carrying the story. Acknowledge their **pain** and validate their perspective.
3. Release: Gently remind them: "We don't have to carry this anymore."

Like physical healing, emotional healing isn't linear. The wound may reopen, and the process may need to be repeated. But with each effort, you grow stronger and more **resilient**.

Building Resilience

Healing doesn't mean erasing the wound. Just as a healed bone develops a callus that makes it stronger than before, emotional healing creates **resilience**. The **trauma** becomes part of your story, but it no longer defines you. Instead, it serves as a source of **strength**, **wisdom**, and **compassion**.

Closing Thoughts-Time doesn't heal wounds—it never has, and it never will. At best, it allows **pain** to lay dormant, waiting for a trigger to resurface it. True healing happens through active engagement with your inner world. As the **observer**, you have the power to guide your wounded villagers toward wholeness, one step at a time.

Healing isn't about erasing the past; it's about integrating it into a **stronger**, more **resilient** self. So, let me ask you: "Which villager is carrying your **pain**? And what will you do to help them heal?"

The staff is in your hands. Healing begins with you.

Reflective Questions

1. Which emotional wound do you feel has remained unhealed in your life, and how has it shaped your reactions or behaviors?
2. What steps can you take as the **observer** to actively engage with the villager carrying your **pain**?
3. What story or narrative is a specific villager—like **fear**, **shame**, or **grief**—holding onto, and how can you challenge or reframe it?
4. What would active healing look like for you?

"There is a crack in everything. That's how the light gets in."

– Leonard Cohen

"We are what we pretend to be, so we must be careful about what we pretend to be."

– Kurt Vonnegut

Chapter 27

- Honorable Mentions -
(The Villagers You Shouldn't Ignore)

In every village, there are voices that might not always take center stage, but their presence is vital. These villagers quietly shape your experience, whether through gentle encouragement, subtle **sabotage**, or the occasional burst of insight. Let's shine a spotlight on some of these honorable mentions and give them the voice they deserve.

The Villager of Overthinking (Unease)
Overthinking is one of the most subtle and pervasive villagers in your emotional village. This villager often operates under the guise of *helping you prepare* or *protecting you from making mistakes.* While preparation and caution can be valuable, overthinking takes these qualities and amplifies them to the point of paralysis, wasting your energy and time. Overthinking can leave you spinning in circles, questioning every move, and often leaves you feeling exhausted and uncertain.

Reversible and Irreversible Changes: A Tool for Clarity
One way to address the villager of overthinking is by introducing a practical tool from science: the concept of *reversible* and *irreversible* changes. In science, a reversible change is one where the process can be undone—for example, when water is heated into vapor and then cooled back into liquid. An irreversible change, on the other hand, creates a permanent transformation, such as when water and concrete mix to form a solid that cannot be returned to its original state.

This same principle can be applied to life and business decisions. Many decisions we overthink fall into the category of reversible changes.

- **Life Example (Reversible):** Moving to a new city for a job is a reversible change. If it doesn't work out, you can likely move back or find a different job in the same city. Overthinking here wastes your energy, as the decision is not permanent.

- **Life Example (Irreversible):** Deciding to have a child is an irreversible change. Once the child is born, there's no going back. This decision warrants deep thought and deliberation because it has permanent consequences.
- **Business Example (Reversible):** Purchasing an investment property at a price where you can easily resell it without financial harm is a reversible decision. It allows you flexibility if the investment doesn't work out.
- **Business Example (Irreversible):** Investing all your capital into a risky business idea with no way to recover your funds if it fails would be an irreversible decision. Such decisions require careful thought and planning.

This tool can help you quickly categorize whether a decision warrants significant attention or whether it's safe to move forward without unnecessary overthinking.

Why We Overthink

Often, the villager of overthinking is accompanied by other villagers like fear, shame, guilt, or disrespect. If you stop and ask, *"Who's talking?"*, you might notice that overthinking is rarely a lone actor—it's usually fueled by deeper emotions:

1. **Fear:** Fear of failure, rejection, or embarrassment can make even reversible decisions feel paralyzing.
2. **Shame:** The fear of making a mistake and feeling unworthy or judged often drives overthinking.
3. **Guilt:** A sense of responsibility to avoid letting others down can lead to over-analyzing simple choices.
4. **Disrespect:** Feeling like your decisions aren't valued or respected by others may cause you to overcompensate by trying to make the "perfect" choice.

By identifying the underlying emotion fueling your overthinking, you can gain control of the staff.

A Reminder from the Observer
When the villager of overthinking starts to take over, remember this: decisions are rarely as critical or final as they seem.
Ask yourself:
- *"Is this decision reversible or irreversible?"*
- *"If it's reversible, what is the worst that could happen if I make a mistake?"*

Most of the time, the worst-case scenario is manageable, and the decision is reversible. By giving yourself permission to move forward without perfection, you can quiet the villager of overthinking and trust in the observer's ability to handle whatever comes next.

The Villager of Comparison
This villager loves to peek over the fence at what others are doing. They point out how successful someone else looks, how perfect their life appears, or how far ahead in life they seem to be. While their intentions might stem from a desire to motivate, their whispers often lead to feelings of inadequacy and disconnection.

How to Handle Them:
- Remind this villager that **comparison** is the thief of **joy**.
- Focus on your own progress instead of measuring yourself against others.
- Practice **gratitude** for what you have and the path you're on.

The Villager of Perfectionism
The villager of **perfectionism** has one goal: to make everything flawless. While this might sound admirable, their relentless standards often paralyze progress and create unnecessary stress. They tend to hold the staff with a tight grip, refusing to let go until everything is "just right."

How to Handle Them:
- Embrace the mantra: "Done is better than perfect."
- Celebrate small wins and progress, even if the outcome isn't ideal.
- Remind this villager that imperfection is part of being human.

The Villager of Gratitude

This villager often goes unnoticed, quietly tending to the garden of appreciation in your village. They encourage you to notice the beauty in the small things, the **kindness** of others, and the simple **joys** of life. When they step forward, they can transform even the darkest days into moments of clarity and **peace**.

How to Nurture Them:
- Start or end your day by listing three things you're **grateful** for.
- Pause during **stressful** moments to acknowledge something good in your life.
- Share your **gratitude** with others—it strengthens relationships and spreads positivity.

The Villager of Curiosity

This villager is the adventurous one, always eager to explore, ask questions, and learn something new. They thrive on discovery and remind you that the unknown isn't something to fear—it's something to embrace.

How to Nurture Them:
- Ask more "what if" and "why not" questions in your daily life.
- Try something new, no matter how small—a hobby, a recipe, or a route home.
- Let **curiosity** guide you toward growth and adaptability.

The Villager of Fear of Change
Change is inevitable, but this villager resists it with every ounce of their being. They like things to stay the same, even when those things no longer serve you. Their voice is rooted in **fear**, but beneath that **fear** is a desire to protect the village from uncertainty.

How to Reassure Them:
- Break changes into smaller, manageable steps to reduce **overwhelm**.
- Reflect on past changes you've navigated successfully—this villager will take comfort in knowing you've handled uncertainty before.
- Emphasize that change isn't about losing—it's about evolving.

The Villager of Shame
The villager of **shame** is the shadowy figure in your village, always pointing out where you've fallen short or made mistakes. They thrive on keeping you small, convincing you that you're unworthy of love, respect, or success.

How to Confront Them:
- Separate your actions from your **identity**: You are not your mistakes.
- Practice **self-compassion** and talk to yourself as you would a dear friend.
- Remember, **shame's** purpose is not to define you—it's a signal to reflect and grow.

The Villager of Play
This villager reminds you that life isn't all about responsibilities and **stress**. They encourage laughter, creativity, and fun, urging you to let loose and reconnect with your inner child.

How to Invite Them Forward:
- Schedule time for hobbies, games, or activities that bring you **joy**.
- Spend time with people who make you laugh and feel lighthearted.
- Remind yourself that play isn't a luxury—it's a necessity for a balanced life.

Final Thoughts on the Honorable Mentions

These villagers may not always demand attention, but their roles are essential for a thriving, harmonious village. Whether it's learning to quiet the villager of **comparison**, embracing the villager of **play**, or nurturing the villager of **gratitude**, giving these voices space to speak helps you lead a more balanced and fulfilling life.

Each villager offers a unique perspective and lesson. When you listen to them and integrate their insights, you deepen your connection to yourself and the world around you.

Reflective Questions:

1. Which of these villagers resonates with you the most right now?
2. How can you give that villager a stronger voice in your daily life?
3. What steps can you take to balance the needs of these honorable mentions within your village?

Chapter 28

- Reclaiming the Staff and Leading Your Village Forward -

Throughout this book, we've explored the intricacies of your inner village. You've met your villagers—those distinct parts of your psyche representing every emotion, thought, and memory you've ever experienced. Some villagers, like **joy** or **curiosity**, bring light and energy to the village. Others, like **fear**, **shame**, or **grief**, often operate in the shadows, carrying heavy burdens that influence your reactions in ways you may not immediately recognize.

You've also come to understand your role as the **observer**—the leader standing atop the cliff, holding the staff that represents **balance** and **control**. This staff is your anchor, your symbol of **self-leadership** and **self-trust**. When you hold it, you guide your village with clarity and purpose. But when it falls into the hands of unruly villagers, **chaos** ensues. **Fear** may stir **panic**. **Anger** may lead to rash decisions. **Self-doubt** may paralyze progress. Your ultimate task as the **observer** is to reclaim the staff when it's lost and use it to lead your village forward.

The Chaos of an Unled Village

Imagine a village where the staff is constantly changing hands. **Fear** grabs it during moments of uncertainty, **anger** seizes it in the heat of a conflict, and **shame** holds onto it after a perceived failure. Without a steady leader, the village becomes reactive and disorganized. Decisions are driven by impulse rather than intention, and the villagers pull in different directions, leaving you drained and overwhelmed.

This is what happens when the **observer** is absent. The staff—your power to lead—falls into the hands of villagers who, while well-meaning, lack the perspective to guide the village effectively. They're doing what they think is best, but their methods often lead more to **chaos** than to **harmony**.

Taking Back the Staff

Reclaiming the staff is not about suppressing your villagers or pretending their voices don't matter. Each villager has a purpose, even the disruptive ones. **Fear** may be trying to protect you from danger. **Anger** may be defending a **boundary**. Even **guilt** and **shame** carry lessons meant to guide you toward growth. Taking back the staff means acknowledging these villagers without letting them **control** you.

When you take back the staff:
1. You Listen with **Compassion**:
    Every villager deserves to be heard. By understanding their motives, you can address their concerns without being overtaken by them.
2. You Respond Instead of React:
    The **observer** chooses thoughtful, intentional responses rather than impulsive reactions.
3. You Focus on the Present:
    Instead of being lost in the past or the future, you guide your village through the here and now.
4. You Build Self-Trust:
    Holding the staff isn't just about **control**—it's about trusting yourself to lead with balance and purpose.

Empowerment through Self-Compassion

Leadership isn't about perfection—it's about presence. There will be moments when you lose the staff, when villagers **overwhelm** you, or when **self-doubt** creeps in. These are not failures; they're opportunities to grow. Leading your village requires **self-compassion**, the ability to **forgive** yourself for missteps, and the willingness to try again.

Remember: even the most challenging villagers, like **shame** or **fear**, are part of you. Embracing them with **love** and **understanding**, rather than **rejection** or **suppression**, is how you create harmony within your village.

Food for Thought:

The Parable of the Two Wolves

An old Cherokee chief was teaching his grandson about life. He said, "A fight is going on inside me. It is a terrible fight, and it is between two wolves. One is evil—he is **anger, envy, sorrow, regret, greed, arrogance, self-pity, guilt, resentment, inferiority, lies, false pride, superiority**, and **ego**. The other is good—he is **joy, peace, love, hope, serenity, humility, kindness, benevolence, empathy, generosity, truth, compassion**, and **faith**." The grandson thought about it and asked, "Which wolf will win?" The old chief simply replied, "The one you feed."

This parable beautifully illustrates the inner conflict between our positive and negative emotions. In the context of your inner village, the wolves represent different villagers—some embodying **anger, resentment**, or **self-doubt**, and others representing **joy, compassion**, or **confidence**. As the **observer**, you have the power to choose which villagers to nurture and which to gently redirect. Feeding the "good wolf" means consciously focusing on positive thoughts and actions, empowering the villagers that contribute to your well-being and harmony. Conversely, dwelling on negative emotions feeds the "evil wolf," allowing those disruptive villagers to dominate. Remember, the aspects of yourself that prevail are the ones you choose to cultivate. By mindfully directing your attention and energy, you can lead your inner village toward **balance**.

*May this book remind you
that you are not alone,
that your story matters, and that even in the chaos of
emotions, there is a leader within you — a quiet observer
to guide you back to yourself.*

*This is for you. You belong.
You are enough.
And you are worth every moment of healing.*

- Chris Hinton

"The best way to predict your future is to create it."

– Abraham Lincoln

Acknowledgments

This book could not have come to life without the unwavering support and inspiration of those around me. To my family and friends, thank you for your belief in me and your encouragement along the way. You gave this project the strength to grow into something truly meaningful.

To my clients, past and present: you've taught me as much as I've ever offered you. Your courage to face challenges and your desire for growth have inspired much of what is written here. .

A special thank you to the philosophers, writers, and therapists who have guided my own journey. Your wisdom has helped shape my understanding of human emotions and the universal struggles we share.

To you, the reader: Thank You!
By picking up this book, you've chosen to take a step toward better understanding yourself and the world around you. That choice is such a profound act of courage and self-love, and I hope you feel proud of it.
If this book has impacted you, sparked a change in your perspective,
or given you tools to harmonize your village,
I humbly ask you to share it with others. Pass it along to a friend, a loved one, or anyone who might need it. Healing happens one conversation at a time, and perhaps this book can inspire a conversation
that creates meaningful change.

Thank you for allowing me to share this journey with you. My deepest hope is that these pages serve as a guide and companion on your path toward self-discovery and growth.

With gratitude,
Christopher Robin Hinton